On Rules

On Rules

Gherardo Colombo

Translated by Elisabetta Zoni
With an introduction by René Foqué

AUP / Comenius

First published as *Sulle regole* in March 2008 by Giangiacomo Feltrinelli
Editore, Milan, Italy
© Giangiacomo Feltrinelli Editore, 2008

Translated by: Elisabetta Zoni

This book is published in collaboration with :

omenius

Cover illustration: Giorgio Lotti

Cover design: Rob Wadman
Lay-out: Crius Group, Hulshout

Amsterdam University Press English-language titles are distributed in the US
and Canada by the University of Chicago Press.

ISBN	978 94 6298 194 2
e-ISBN	978 90 4853 174 5 (pdf)
e-ISBN	978 90 4853 175 2 (ePub)
NUR	740

© Gherardo Colombo / Amsterdam University Press B.V., Amsterdam 2015
Introduction: © René Foqué

Introduction
Gherardo Colombo's Concern for the Democratic State under the Rule of Law: A Work in Progress

René Foqué[1]

In 2008 Gherardo Colombo published the book *Sulle regole* (*On Rules*) in which he explains why it is so important for Italian society to repair its fractured relationship with rules and rule-following.[2] The book quickly grew to become a bestseller having, surprisingly, a very persuasive impact among younger generations. This formed the basis of his many public lectures and debates. These were not only directed at school-aged children and young (and also not so young) adults. Colombo became more and more convinced that constitutional citizenship must be cultivated from a very young age. So together with Anna Sarfatti, a specialist in child education, he published in 2009, one year after *Sulle regole*, a short children's book which explained in a pedagogically expert, elegant way the Italian Constitution, its letter and spirit, to elementary school children.[3] The practical outcome of this book has been to foster in many young people more personal autonomy and greater societal engagement.

Sulle regole formulates the grounding principles of Colombo's further work. It is an impressive book which immediately draws the reader into conversation. That is the case because it draws its inspiration from three important perspectives which frame at the same time the particular form of professional self-consciousness, one which characterises the writer himself. This book is written by an author who is able to translate his practical experience as a long-serving magistrate during one of the most turbulent periods in recent

Italian history into profound, social and philosophical reflections on that practice, and ultimately to connect very personal choices to it.[4]

1. Tackling Systemic Corruption: A Seemingly Impossible Task

In March 1981, the Milan investigating magistrate Gherardo Colombo was tasked with the murder investigation of the lawyer Giorgio Ambrosoli. The trail pointed all too quickly to the shady practices of the banker Michele Sindona, already well-known to the police.[5] In a very short time Sindona had positioned himself as one of the central figures of Italian high finance. This had not occurred, however, without a list of dubious contacts and ties to the mafia. Sindona was in regular contact with mafia bosses, and the mid 1950s saw him start his long-term and close involvement with the American mafia via the equally unsavoury Joe Adonis. In that same period his presence was signalled in Palermo at a meeting of the heads of the American mafia and the Sicilian *Cosa Nostra*. At that meeting, as would later come to light, they worked out a comprehensive strategy for the international trade in weapons and drugs.

As a banker, Sindona pursued a very active commercial policy. Towards the end of the 1950s he had invested in the *Instituto per le Opere Religiose* that was led by the equally shady Cardinal Marcinkus. This was the first step in his building up of an unnaturally powerful financial empire in the 1960s, to which the later notorious *Banco Ambrosiano* of Roberto Calvi belonged.

Michele Sindona was also politically very active. He was connected with the fascist leader Junio Valerio Borghese, one of the more recent founders of the ultra-right *Fronte Nazionale* responsible for a failed coup in 1970. He stood in the good graces of the then prime minister Giulio Andreotti, as well as of the American diplomatic mission in Rome.

That Michele Sindona was the spider in the middle of a financial and political web in post-war Italy is clear, just as there existed as a consequence little doubt if any in suspecting close ties between above-ground and underworld activities. But how sinister was this web of power and how influential was it in reality?

During the course of their investigation of the many radiations of Sindona's web, Gherardo Colombo and his colleague Giuliano Turone came upon one astonishing find after another. In the offices of a certain Licio Gelli, they found the members list of the secretive Freemason's lodge *Propoganda Due (P2)* containing about 1000 names.[6] It quickly became apparent that this in fact concerned a highly suspicious group of individuals with plans to subvert the regime and with a highly organised system of bribery and government corruption. On that list were names from the upper echelons of the Italian judiciary, the army, the police, political parties, and major companies. Colombo and his colleagues were immediately convinced that they had stumbled upon a network of corruption of immense proportions.[7] The Italian state seemed to be teetering on the precipice of falling into a totally rotten, corrupted state. Moreover there appeared to be a number of ties between the Catholic Church and that corrupted Italian system.[8]

2.   Mani Pulite: Illusion and Disillusion

A large-scale investigation was launched by the Milan prosecutor's office into corrupt practices, extending even up to the higher reaches of the state. Thus an investigation was also started into the activities of a then up and coming Silvio Berlusconi, whose name too was included on the P2 members list. A widespread practice of bribery, illicit party finance, and hush money came to light, implicating increasingly more well-placed figures in Italian politics, banking, and business circles. All hope for restoring the democratic state under the rule of law and a public service beyond reproach came to rest on the integrity of the judicial branch. A policy of *mani pulite*, of 'clean hands' would now take charge. They were the ones, Gherardo Colombo and his colleagues (including Antonio di Pietro), who represented the hopes for the coming of integrity and true rule of law in the state. The work of *mani pulite* – even from a European perspective on the judiciary as well – stood as a yet unseen form of voluntarism. These magistrates offered a powerful affirmation of what the Italian philosopher Antonio Gramsci once called 'the optimism of the will' in opposition to the pessimism of rational analyses and prognoses.

Even so, *mani pulite* would reach its limits, and in the end it would appear to have had little effect. Alberto Vannucci, a professor at the University of Pisa, has recently produced a penetrating analysis of what he calls 'the legacy of *mani pulite*'.[9] Relying on empirical data, he has concluded to his dismay that the perception of government corruption, and thus the fight against it, is disappearing from the public eye. According to Vannucci, this does not mean however that systemic corruption has been rooted out or has been by and large eradicated. Quite the opposite. His conclusion is as hard as it is clear. "The *mani pulite* inquiries courageously exposed, but could not solve the issue of widespread corruption in Italy. An enduring improvement in the quality of public ethics would have required the specific interest and consequent action of leading political actors, or strong and enduring social support for an anti-corruption agenda. Neither condition, however, has ever been realized."[10]

It has to be acknowledged that the judicial branch, albeit formally and legally independent of the political branch, is and remains nevertheless dependent in certain practical ways on that political branch which is in charge. And that political class did not, does not, share with the magistrates of *mani pulite* a like resolve to dispose fully and finally of those mechanisms of corrupting influence. To the contrary, it constitutes a part of the mechanism and thus has every interest in maintaining the status quo. The Milan judges must have indeed experienced that in the ways in which their work was hindered. One significant element in that was, for example, the decision to remove the whole file on the P2 lodge from the Milan prosecutor's office, and transfer the case to Rome. That move led largely to the fragmentation and evaporation of any effective investigation and prosecution, and the whole case more or less disappeared from public awareness, which attention had fuelled the enthusiasm driving *mani pulite*.[11] Justice seemed doomed to ineffectiveness by a wave of laws and regulations intended to stand in the way of an effective, efficacious investigation or, worse still, which decriminalised conduct previously declared illegal.[12] In short, the Italian government machine was definitely characterised by a considerable ability to arrange the status quo and to perpetuate various types of illegal practices, as well as to finesse the administrative structures and informal channels needed for all that. Thus it appeared that all the old corrupt practices would continue to cast the dark hearts of their shadows long into the future.[13]

3. A Lack of Constitutional Culture in Political and Civil Society

Gherardo Colombo gradually came to realise – and very clearly – how ineffective the administration of justice was, in spite of the dynamic of *mani pulite*. Looking back on that period, he has noted that not one law or decree was passed during those years to facilitate investigations and prosecutions, or to make the various forms of corrupt practices less attractive. No measures were taken to reassess current procedures and improve them where necessary. And finally, no action was taken against the unscrupulous, tainted by corruption, to remove them from the public service. Quite the opposite, many politicians instead became complicit by offering protection for notorious mafiosi.[14] When all of this is duly added up, the net result cannot but be calculated as a negative: even *mani pulite* would stall as ineffective and would be destined to fail beyond a certain point.

But it was not only the political classes who conspired to maintain this corrupt situation. Even on the part of civil society there was a good deal amiss. The citizenry had little concern in the end for public system ethics and, despite initial and superficial sympathies for *mani pulite*, offered little by way of strong and concrete support for sanitising their public authorities. This means that there existed hardly any democratic support for strengthening the democratic state and the rule of law. Colombo analyses Italian civil society as a vertically functioning society (*la società verticale*).[15] A vertical society is characterised by a command hierarchy, by the intimidation of lower levels by the higher ones, and by the dilemma of obedience-disobedience. Citizens in this kind of society have a dysfunctional relationship with the rule of law state, which for them can be nothing other than an authoritarian state exercising its power over citizens through the instrument of law. Practically speaking this latter aspect leads to citizens having a distorted view of rules and, in particular, of what it is to follow rules.

In a vertical society there is no place for a highly developed, communal sense of responsibility for the general good underlying citizenship. And it is even less the case for any sense or insight that a democratic state under the rule of law is not some power hanging over them, but instead represents an ordered form of community life based on the equality of all before and in the law. It is just this insight, by contrast, that stands as one of the central pillars to a horizontal society (*la società orrizontale*).[16]

Ultimately this all comes down to what conception of democracy would seem to prevail in the vertical society of Italy.[17] Democracy here is reduced to a mechanism to legitimate in effect the excesses of top-down power: the dictatorship of the elected leader or of the elected majority. The person who receives a majority of the votes cast – even if by the narrowest of differences brought about by a solitary ballot – may therefore claim legitimacy for all his actions and decisions. To put it another way, democracy in this fashion raises the *vox populi* to the highest power, under which also stand the institutions and principles of a rule of law state. We see this precisely in the stance of Silvio Berlusconi who ignored the ruling of the Italian Constitutional Court of 13 January 2011. The Court had declared unconstitutional a law which set up the so called 'legitimate inability' of the Prime Minister, allowing him to avoid appearing before the courts by reason of pressing matters of state. But for Berlusconi, the operative proposition was that the *vox populi* was above the law, and certainly ought to supersede a decision of the Constitutional Court which body was not legitimated by the will of the people. In short, the Berlusconi doctrine stands for the proposition that the rule of law here unjustifiably disregarded the workings of democracy.[18] A like authoritarian conception of the democratic state forms an ideal seedbed for corruption and for a dirty and opaque culture of governance, one which is staffed in the end by unscrupulous servants of a power that is only interested in its own advantage and profit.

In the horizontal society, on the other hand, the rule of law and the democratic state are inseparable complements. The former Minister of Justice of the Netherlands, Ernst Hirsch Ballin, has recently given cogent expression to this, and his remarks are unreservedly and directly pertinent for the Italian situation. "Democracy and the rule of law are not separable. If there is but one task, one goal that must count for politics, it is not just to accept, 'to respect', but also to will with effect, to bring forth."[19]

Not only the Italian political class, but also Italian civil society suffers from a double deficit: a democratic one and a rule of law one. The reinstitution of the culture of a democratic state under the rule of law will be an undertaking over the long-term; but it is more than a necessary undertaking. The democratic state must once again, more than two and half centuries after Montesquieu's constitutionalism, be revitalised as a constitutionally anchored and structured form of governance and community.

4. The Importance of a Constitution: a Formative Project

Here we see the insight and the new ambition of Gherardo Colombo, one which led him to leave the judiciary in 2007. This does not mean, however, that he had lost hope for any restoration of a democratic state under the rule of law.[20] His voluntarism, fuelled by an optimism for the future, continued to motivate him with fresh inspiration and to further action. He would pursue the struggle, but on different fronts. From 2007 onwards, he began to devote more energy to education and teaching. Colombo firmly believes that an enduring democratic state under the rule of law in Italy can be reconstructed only by laying out the constitution, not only in letter but in spirit as well, for the younger generation from elementary schools to universities. Only in this way can civil society be once again brought back to democratic health. Virtually every day, tirelessly, Colombo is lecturing and speaking in public, as well as also writing lucid, clear articles analysing the importance of the rule of law for a stable and balanced democratic state, one in which its citizens can make truly free and which can foster once again a real sense of community and ethical self-respect. In doing so, Colombo brings a classical Athenian view into practice regarding one of the necessary conditions for a democratic 'horizontal' society, one not reliant on an external authority, but rather on an internal capacity of citizens working for and with one another in a shared concern for the *res publica*. In place of the authoritarian myth of the supposed *vox populi*, as if the people were a single person, a 'sir and sire', we have a diversity of active and participatory citizens. The Athens of antiquity knew it well: no *demokratia* without *paideia*, without education and training.[21] Colombo takes this very seriously, and travels literally to every corner of the country to bring this about.

5. The Philosophical Underpinnings: What is it to Follow a Rule?

Colombo's educational project should in no way be understood as merely the naïve initiative of a 'believer' who is trying against better judgement to deal with and forget being a disillusioned judge. Quite the opposite. Colombo's driving force is his understanding of a (legal) philosophical idea of what law and rules mean, and what it is to follow rules.

The Austrian-British philosopher Ludwig Wittgenstein has given penetrating consideration to this question in his *Philosophical Investigations*.[22] Complying with a rule is, for him, a complex and intersubjective practice. "It is not possible to obey a rule 'privately'," says Wittgenstein. Or to put it another way, to follow a rule does not mean an 'on your own account' obedience to a rule-issuing authority, as is the case in a vertical society. To follow a rule is to enter into a social practice which is shared by others and which refers to a common understanding of a shared world.[23]

The citizen *qua* responsible and autonomous moral actor in the public domain is more than, and different from, a 'centre of monological consciousness', to borrow a phrase from the Canadian philosopher Charles Taylor. A citizen is an acting, thinking person-in-a-community, "engaged in practices, as a being who acts in and on a world."[24] In a democratic state under the rule of law, a citizen is an actor integrated into a society which can provide sense and meaning to his actions. In this regard, Taylor speaks of an "integrated, nonindividual agent".[25]

Against this backdrop, following a rule is conceived as entering into, or participating in, a social practice. In the old Roman law sense of the word, *regula* meant a standardised practice, condensed into a precept, of behaving properly with others. Together with this tradition of thinking about rules, we can say that rules always refer in one way or another to the narrative of customs or usages which make a community meaningful and recognisable for everyone.

In a democratic state under the rule of law, rules are not to be understood as the intimidating commands that are imposed from above onto the citizens below. That sort of conception of rules belongs to a vertically structured and deferential economy of commands (*bevelshuishouding*). In that order there is no place for autonomous and participatory citizenship. Only in a horizontal economy of deliberation (*onderhandelingshuishouding*),[26] can such a form of citizenship flourish, supported by a shared *habitus* as a common reference point.[27]

Rules function in our lives in the first place not as the causal reasons for regularity, nor as top-down imposed commands or prohibitions, but as "patterns of reasons for action".[28] They are dialogical and relational in nature, as Montesquieu reiterated in his monumental *De l'Esprit des Lois*. They prescribe the necessary relationships, and customs and practices which must be observed if a system of governance wishes to remain moderate, and a society, decent and pluralistic.

All this constitutes the philosophical underpinning for Colombo's argument for a horizontal society under the direction of a balanced constitution. The impotence of the Italian judiciary, even during the short-lived dynamic of *mani pulite*, has demonstrated in all fullness that integrity and decency cannot be realised unless politics and civil society are thoroughly infused with those elements.

Seen thus, Colombo's project represents a necessary, needed actualisation of the democratic state under the rule of law. Having a democratic state under the rule of law is indeed no sinecure, but demands constant care and attention, including very much in the first place care to teach and pass on those principles. This is true not only for Italy, but especially also for the Low Countries.

6. Food for Thought and for Action: Constitutionalism and Leadership

Such is this adventure of Gherardo Colombo in its threefold character – from practical experience at the very heart of justice, through profound reflection on the political and philosophical assumptions at play there, to deeply considered choices and active engagement – that it surely must move us to reflection of our own, and should inspire us in making our own decisions. His work not only concerns the Italian context, but also addresses in particular, for the rest of Europe and the Low Countries too, the very core of the democratic state and the rule of law.

Primo, there is the matter of learning democracy – of teaching citizenship and learning to become citizens. Our modern society can be characterised as an abstract and highly commercialised community in which it is not so much the co-operation between citizens at the forefront as it is a general competitiveness. As a result, social cohesion would appear to have become more diffuse, and can no longer be taken for granted. A sense of recognition of, and a pride and duty in, being 'a citizen' – a necessary prerequisite in the Aristotelian vision for real liberty – can likewise no longer be taken as a given. In its 1992 report, the Netherlands *Wetenschappelijke Raad voor het Regeringsbeleid* (a think-tank of the Dutch government, established under the direction of the Leiden professor Van Gunsteren) argued forcefully and persuasively that a sense of pride and duty as a citizen in a pluralistic society can only arise 'in the actual free intercourse among pluralities in the public sphere' [my translation] and not through a rather demagogic and thus free-standing appeal to the good intentions and goodwill of the private sphere, nor by abstract rules imposed top-down.[29] In Colombo's terms, it is not the vertical society but the horizontal one that advances liberty and decency. The sense of being 'a citizen' – just like democracy itself – can only arise and flourish in actually experiencing and practising citizenship itself. For that reason we need to provide every opportunity to facilitate and intensify this hands-on experience. And in doing that, we should not strengthen or develop competitiveness among citizens, but rather find our way to an enduring culture of mutual co-operation in the realisation that we all are 'co-builders of a common world'.[30]

Secondo, it is not by coincidence that Hannah Arendt linked the idea that we are all builders of a common world, a phrase coined by her, not only to the idea of democratic political responsibility, but moreover to the issue of rights to liberty and the fundamental rights which are the necessary prerequisites for human liberty and dignity. Those rights are guaranteed in, and protected by, a constitution. An enduring constitutional mindset in both officials and citizens is therefore an absolute necessity for a decent society based upon the liberty of its citizens. This is why Colombo too attaches so much importance to both young and old understanding and accepting the constitution as a mode of living together.[31] A sense of recognition of, and a pride and duty in, being 'a citizen' presume a care and concern for public matters and a loyalty to the principles and institutions of the democratic state under the rule of law, as are anchored in a constitution.

Terzo, interpreting the constitution and ensuring compliance with it ought to be, in any democratic state under the rule of law, independent from the political pretensions of the moment, as well as from administrative opportunism in managing affairs during times of crisis. The independence of the judicial branch is therefore a cornerstone to any democratic state under the rule of law. The story of Gherardo Colombo proves, with its forceful and cogent arguments in fact and in principle, just how much the legislative and executive branches can undermine the effectiveness of justice. The position of a constitutional court in light of that is certainly deserving of reconsideration, as is the issue of judicial constitutional review in those circumstances. An independent court, more so than a parliament, ought to play a central role.

Quarto, all this implicates what we might term the 'principles of good leadership'. Gherardo Colombo allows us to see in his own life what here is of prime importance. His work has in large measure the character of critical and yet constructive reflection on one's own engagement and on the context in which that engagement occurs. He is, in the true sense of the word, a 'reflective practitioner'. Good leadership is not possible without this capacity for reflection. Or more forcefully still, leadership without reflection risks in the circumstances degenerating into intolerable and even illegal action. That is, for example, what Hannah Arendt described in her account of the Eichmann trial. She described his conduct as the 'banality of evil', governed as it was by a 'thoughtlessness', the absence of reflection. Thus any and every value orientation becomes impossible. But not only a reflective capacity, but also an authenticity and the courage to set out against the current are important for good leadership – as Colombo himself exemplifies. It is striking also how often Colombo recognises the importance of envisioning not just the likely, but also and especially the possible. Knowledge without imagination, as the philosopher Kant on occasion says, is empty knowledge. Literature can offer here a significant source of inspiration for good leadership and citizenship.[32] Good leadership ought to help building up the horizontal society further, to facilitate uniting people even where they hold diverse and conflicting views.

Given these considerations, Colombo brings to light in what he has written and in what he is doing the inescapable paradox to good leadership. Otherwise than what the term at first glance might lead us to suspect, leadership in a horizontal society has little to do with the top-down exercise of power, or getting one's own way as in the vertical society. Colombo's case for a horizontal society raises once again, what in the democratic tradition was for example given expression by Aristotle and developed further by more recent and modern thinkers as Montesquieu and Hannah Arendt, the point that political power and leadership do not represent the ability to impose your will on another, but rather the capacity to think together, deliberate together, and act together in the articulation and generation of the common good. And that is why a certain modesty in the appreciation of others, of being inquisitive rather than immediately having some sort of retort ready to hand, is an indispensable ingredient to living, as the intellectual inheritance of the 17th century thinker and educator Comenius continues to exemplify for us.[33] Before speaking, we need to have listened – listened to others, to our community, to our own conduct and engagement, and to the world in which we live. Seen thus from this perspective, in the modesty and dignity of his educational projects,[34] Gherardo Colombo stands as an impressive teacher and example of good leadership in a horizontal society.

Notes

1. René Foqué is emeritus Professor of Philosophy of Law and Legal Theory at the Faculties of Law of the Catholic University of Leuven and of the Erasmus University of Rotterdam. He teaches at the European InterUniversity Centre for Human Rights and Democratisation in Venice and is a corresponding fellow of the Netherlands Royal Academy of Sciences. He has been for a number of years the academic co-ordinator of the Bologna Law Programme, part of the Comenius European Leadership Course.

2. G. Colombo, *Sulle regole*, Feltrinelli, Milano, 2008.

3. G. Colombo and A. Sarfatti, *Sei Stato tu? La Costituzione attraverso le domande dei bambini*, Salani Editore, Milano, 2009.

4. See further R. Foqué, 'Gherardo Colombo's actualisering van de Italiaanse rechtsstaat in de strijd tegen corruptie: een onvoltooid project', in T. Spapens, M. Groenhuijsen, T. Kooijmans (eds.), *Universalis. Liber Amicorum Cyrille Fijnaut*, Intersentia, Antwerpen/Cambridge, 2011, pp. 91-99. This introduction draws on that previous work.

5. For more detailed information about the figure of Michele Sindona, see for instance C. Stajano, *Un eroe borghese. Il caso dell' avvocato Giorgio Ambrosoli assassinato dalla mafia politica*, Einaudi, Torino, 1991, pp. 44-92.

6. A. Vinci (ed.), *La P2. Nei diari segreti di Tina Anselmi*, Chiarelettere, Milano, 2011; the P2 members list can still be found at, e.g., www.stragi.it/2agost80/iscrittiP2.pdf.

7. G. Colombo, *Il vizio della memoria*, Feltrinelli, Milano, 1996, p. 46 et seq.

8. Extremely informative on the Vatican's role, but also extremely embarrassing for it, is the book by G. Nuzzi, *Vaticano S.p.A.*, Chiarelettere, Milano, 2009, in which not only the highly suspect role of a number of cardinals associated with the central figure of Cardinal Marcinkus is laid out, but also the Vatican's criminal ties to the *Banco Ambrosiano* of Roberto Calvi ('God's banker'!) later found dead under a London bridge, and to the Italian Christian Democrats around the figure of Giulio Andreotti.

9. A. Vannucci, "The Controversial Legacy of '*Mani Pulite*': A Critical Analysis of Italian Corruption and Anti-Corruption Policies", *Bulletin of Italian Politics* 1 (2009) 2, pp. 233-264.

10. Vannucci, *op.cit.*, p. 259.

11. Colombo, *Il vizio della memoria, op.cit.*, pp. 8-10.

12. Vannucci, *op.cit.*, p.242, with reference to the research of P. Davigo and G. Mannozzi, *La corruzione in Italia. Percezione sociale e controllo penale*, Laterza, Roma/Bari, 2007, whose observations brought them to the conclusion that this was truly an instance of a 'funnel effect' casued by a series of cumulative measures as a result of which ultimately only a mere 2% of the accused, held in remand in Italian prisons, were convicted of corruption related offences.

13. Vannucci, *op.cit.*, p. 257.

14. Colombo, *Il vizio della memoria, op.cit.*, p. 154.

15. Colombo, *Sulle regole*, Milano, 2008, pp. 41-47, 59-64.

16. Colombo, *Sulle regole*, *op.cit.*, pp. 48-56, 65-71.

17. Colombo, *Democrazia*, Bollati Boringhieri, Torino, 2011.

18. A. Gibelli, *Berlusconi ou la démocratie autoritaire*, Belin, Paris, 2011, pp. 113-130.

19. E. Hirsch Ballin, 'De rechtsstaat, wachten op een nieuwe dageraad', in *Nederlands Juristen Blad* (2011) 2, pp. 71-73.

20. This cannot be made any more clear and certain than by his recent work, G. Colombo, *Lettera a un figlio su Mani pulite*, Garzanti, Milano, 2015.

21. Of course, this is not to diminish nor ignore the oligarchical characteristics of classical Athenian democracy, nor how those characteristics may have interfered with the proper operation of its democratic ideal.

22. L. Wittgenstein, *Philosophical Investigations*, Basil Blackwell, Oxford, 1953, p. 80 et seq.

23. Ch. Taylor, "To Follow a Rule", in his *Philosophical Arguments*, Harvard University Press, Cambridge (Mass.)/London, 1995, pp. 165-180.

24. Taylor, *op.cit.*, p. 170.

25. Taylor, *op.cit.*, p. 172.

26. I am borrowing the terms '*bevelshuishouding*' and '*onderhandelingshuishouding*' from the Netherlands sociologist Abram de Swaan in his well-known 1979 inagural lecture in Amsterdam, "Uitgaansbeperking en uitgangsangst. Over de verschuiving van bevelshuishouding naar onderhandelingshuishouding", in J. Heilbron and G. de Vries (eds.), *De draagbare De Swaan*, Prometheus, Amsterdam, 2008, pp. 175-208.

27. P. Bourdieu, *Le sens pratique*, Les Éditions de Minuit, Paris, 1980, pp. 58 et seq.

28. Taylor, *op.cit.*, p. 179.

29. H. van Gunsteren, *A Theory of Citizenship. Organizing Plurality in Contemporary Democracies*, Westview Press, Boulder Colorado/Oxford, 1998.

30. The phrase comes from Hannah Arendt, *The Origins of Totalitarianism*, Isaac Deutsch, London, 1951, p. 458.

31. G. Colombo and A. Sarfatti, *Sei Stato tu? La Costituzione attraverso le domande dei bambini*, Salani Editore, Milano, 2009; G. Colombo and F. Marzoli, *Farla franca. La legge è uguale per tutti?*, Longanesi, Milano, 2012; G. Colombo and R. de Monticelli (eds), *La Repubblica*

siamo noi. A scuola di Costituzione con i ragazzi di libertà e giustizia,
Salani Editore, Milano, 2013.

32.   See, e.g., the edition of Dostoevsky's story within a story of the
grand inquisitor from his *The Brothers Karamazov* with comments
by Colombo: F. Dostoevsky, *Il grande Inquisitore*, con G. Colombo,
Il peso della libertà. Una riflessione di Gherardo Colombo, Salani
Editore, Milano, 2010.

33.   H. Woldring, *Jan Amos Comenius. Zijn leven, missie en erfenis*,
Damon, Budel, 2014.

34.   It would not be at all amiss to note here, as illustrating the multi-
faceted nature of Colombo's leadership role, the following: in
addition to his many lectures and publications, Gherardo Colombo
is also the president of the publishing house *Garzanti* and a former
member of the board of directors of the RAI, the Italian public
broadcasting service. In 2010 he established the *Associazione Sulle
Regole* to stimulate further public debate over the constitution and
over the importance to the principle of legality.

Gherardo Colombo: A Short Bibliography

G. Colombo, *Il vizio della memoria*, Feltrinelli, Milano, 1996.

G. Colombo, *Sulle regole*, Feltrinelli, Milano, 2008.

G. Colombo and A. Sarfatti, *Sei Stato tu? La Costituzione attraverso le domande
dei bambini*, Salani Editore, Milano, 2009.

G. Colombo, "Il peso della libertà. Una riflessione di Gherardo Colombo", in:
F. Dostoevskij, *Il grande inquisitore,* (Traduzione di Serena Vitale), Salani
Editore, Milano, 2010.

G. Colombo, *Che cos'è la legalità?*, CD Audio, Luca Sossella Editore, Roma, 2010.

G. Colombo, *Democrazia*, Bollati Boringhieri Editore, Torino, 2011.

G. Colombo, *Il perdono responsabile*, Salani Editore, Milano, 2011.

G. Colombo and F. Marzoli, *Farla franca. La legge è uguale per tutti?*, Longanesi,
Milano, 2012.

G. Colombo and R. de Monticelli (a cura di), *La repubblica siamo noi. A scuola di
Costituzione con I ragazzi di libertà e giustizia*, Salani Editore, Milano, 2013.

G. Colombo, *Lettera a un figlio su Mani Pulite*, Garzanti, Milano, 2015.

G. Colombo and E. Passerini, *Imparare la libertà,* Salani Editore, Milano, 2013

Why?

I left the judiciary after more than 33 years, having worked first as a judge, then as a public prosecutor, and then again as a judge. I resigned because, with investigation after investigation, I became convinced that it would have been impossible for me – from that moment on– to help make the administration of justice less bad than it was. I gradually became convinced that, in order for justice to change, it would instead be useful to intensify what I was already trying to do in my time off from work – visiting schools, universities, parishes, clubs and associations, and any other place where I was invited to talk about the subject of rules. Justice cannot function if the relationship between citizens and rules is sick, painful, marred by lack of communication.

The administration of justice, as a system that involves judges, law courts, lawyers, public prosecutors, prisons, and the people whose lives are affected mostly severely by this system, seems unable to function. Nor is justice, seen as a point of reference, as the foundation of the relationships among the inhabitants of the world, able to perform the function of setting out, even more than checking, what is allowed and what is taboo, benefits and burdens, orders and prohibitions, restrictions and liberties.

Justice cannot function if citizens do not understand the point of rules. If they do not understand it, they tend to get round them when they think they are hard to follow, and to break them when they clash with their will.

In order for justice to function, a change in this relationship is necessary.

I resigned in order to bring my own tiny grain of sand onto the road for change. The following pages are a part of that tiny grain.

Gherardo Colombo

1.   An Imaginary Country

This is an imaginary country.

On a street corner there is a deli. A policeman enters the shop. His task is, among other things, to check the scales. After a couple of innuendos, half sentences, and understanding looks, the policeman goes out with a couple of full shopping bags. He got them for free, and in exchange he did not check anything. The shopkeeper can go on selling the wrapping paper at the same price as the ham. Two floors up, in the same building, a lady is paying the plumber who has just repaired her faucet. "If you want an invoice it will be 120 euro, 90 without invoice, a little discount." "No invoice, I don't need it; thanks for the discount." A few steps away is the tax office. A distinguished gentleman is talking to an official about an alleged tax evasion. After a while, having understood that the other will not refuse, the gentleman slides an envelope full of money into his hands. They exchange a couple more words, shake hands, and say goodbye: the tax evasion has disappeared. A little further there is a bank. A client goes in; he is an account holder. He greets the teller, opens the briefcase he carries with him, and places a series of banknote bundles on the counter. The teller, alerted by the bank director, explains to him how to deposit them avoiding anti-money-laundering measures.

Two blocks away is the courts building (a license for building additional floors has been granted to the company that paid a substantial bribe). A lawyer and a judge are negotiating the outcome of a trial that involves powerful people. In the nearby prison another lawyer is talking to his client, boasting about his connections with the investigating magistrate who is handling the case. "You're in deep trouble, but with an adequate gift to the judge, your freedom is guaranteed." In his office, another lawyer receives sizable 'expense funds' without an invoice, tax-free. A couple of miles away, at the stadium, a football match is being played. The referee blows his whistle, awarding a highly doubtful penalty kick to the home team, from whose managers he had received, days earlier, a beautiful branded watch as a token of appreciation for his expertise. In the evening, in an isolated place, a politician from a major party receives a suitcase from the CEO of the company managing the construction of the subway. It contains all the bribes that were meticulously collected from all the companies involved in the construction work. The person who has now received them phones his colleagues in the other top parties, "See you tomorrow," and the next day the money is divided according to pre-agreed rates, so much per head, with variable percentages depending on the political weight of the party. Late in the evening, on a suburban street, a distinguished gentleman negotiates with a girl 'imported' from a poorer country under false pretences and forced by violence and intimidation to live under conditions not unlike those of a slave.

The following morning, at a civilian hospital, surgeons are implanting heart valves that are later found to be faulty, but whose purchase (once again) was accompanied by bribes. Meanwhile, family doctors are ordering for their patients tests they do not need, to be carried out in private clinics with expenses charged to the Region, or patent medicines by pharma-companies that have invited them to a congress in a well-known seaside resort (an all inclusive week-end for the doctor and his family). In a nearby barracks, the marshal of the orderly room takes home a quarter of beef, all wrapped up to be deep-frozen, which was actually destined for the NCO canteen, while in the command office they are concocting purchase contracts for supplies of doubtful utility, and here too, a deal is struck in exchange for a little cash. Three streets away is a building site. The work supervisor knocks at the office door: he must check that accident prevention measures have been taken in compliance with regulations. They hand him a list of items (helmets, safety belts, anti-slip shoes) along with an envelope (containing money). He fills out a regulation compliance certificate for the building site and goes away. At the retirement planning institute someone is falsifying the computer data of a person who begged him (with an offering) to make him appear professionally older than he is. Without even asking for anything in return, a family doctor issues a sick note after receiving a phone call from a public servant, who has extended his holiday by a few days. The funeral director has made an agreement with the hospital nurses: so much for each exclusive death notice. Meanwhile the filling station attendant has adjusted the fuel nozzles in order to pocket the virtually inconspicuous difference in price per litre, which makes up a pretty penny at the end of the week. Officers of the revenue police are 'softened' by the usual envelope, and their audit of the big company's accounts results in a highly positive report. The brand of the school lunch food was chosen in exchange for money. For money, someone allows narcotics to be smuggled into prison. Advertising and consulting agencies help their clients create black funds, returning part of their service fees in the black. Irreproachable entrepreneurs turn to organised crime to dispose of the toxic and dangerous waste produced by their businesses. In his newspaper, a journalist praises the qualities and virtues of a certain object, after having been adequately encouraged to do so. Some highways have to be built over and over again, because the developer skimped on concrete. Examinations are fixed in order to allow admission to university. Land that should be destined for parks is declared building land (again in exchange for money). Money is paid to receive a license to build a new airport, to gain priority in the supply of railway material, to obtain a place in the cemetery.

Then there's the mafia. There are individuals who, once a month (where the mafia is stronger), visit all the shops and businesses to collect the 'insurance premium against criminal damage', the fee for a 'protection' guaranteed to those who do not refuse to pay. There are individuals who infiltrate institutions, who ask and obtain a share for the mafia in public contracts. Some deal in drugs, others in human beings. There are also (sometimes) people who make such agreements even at low levels: the policeman who tries to get by and receives favours (money, drugs, easy girls) in exchange for turning a blind eye.

Subterfuges, cunning, the use of force, and dishonesty prevail under the cloak of equal laws for everybody and respect for every basic right. The people (not necessarily a handful) who abide by the formal laws are overtaken every day by those who do not observe them.

Contents

Part III Towards a Horizontal Society

Part IV How Do We Get There?

Part I
The Ambiguities of Justice

2.   Law and Justice

Even if some people think the opposite, rules cannot be done without, because people cannot live together without applying them, even if unwittingly.

A rule is the other side of living together – they are two sides of the same coin. This can be tested empirically: it is impossible to meet unless we follow the same rules for measuring time. We cannot communicate unless we follow shared language rules. Often, if not always, contacts between people have specific rules: sitting at a table, attending a lecture, going to school (just to name a few), all these activities have specific rules.

By the same token, it can be observed that every kind of association, community or faction – a religious order, a bowls club, a cinema club, the mafia, and so on – is based on rules.

Rules, laws, and legality are the words people use most frequently when confronted with facts, dramatic events and contradictions relating to human relationships. They are neutral terms, whose meaning can vary indefinitely depending on the content they express.

To be clear, it was law that allowed slavery, or discrimination against Jews. Laws still provide for the death penalty today in many states. Likewise, it is law that establishes the freedom and equality of citisens, and it is law that bans capital punishment in most states today. To give a real meaning to such words as 'rules', 'law', and 'rule of law', we need to look at their content. But how can we evaluate this content, and therefore know what it means to abide by the laws or, as it is generally referred to, the 'rule of law'?

3.   Laws Differing in Time and Space

The expression 'rule of law' alone only refers to the attitude of citizens towards law. It is a neutral term, and in order to be filled with meaning, it needs further clarification.

Laws, the legal system, rules, can differ greatly and even contradict each other depending on the historical period and the countries in which they are in force.

Not long ago (in 1938), Italy passed a series of laws, called 'racial' because they differentiated citizens according to their ethnic group, and introducing heavy discrimination against Jews and, in significantly less restrictive terms, against other groups. Among other things, the laws forbade people of Jewish origin to be employed in the public sector, in particular as school teachers, and also forbade children and young people of Jewish origin from attending school. When the Fascist regime fell, those laws were repealed. The Italian system was equally legal before and after the passing and the repeal of the racial laws, but the difference is evident.

Less than a century earlier (in 1865) a thirteenth amendment to the United States Constitution (which had come into force in 1787) became necessary to mark the end of slavery in that country. Until then, in the United States of America it was legal for a person to be the property of another person. Afterwards, the converse became legal. Legality existed before the Constitution was modified, and after the amendment.

Similarly, today a system in which capital punishment is applied because there are laws that provide for it, is as legal as a system where it is not because that penalty was abolished.

The fact that such different – and even contradictory – varieties of 'legality' can exist, shows that an unconditional appreciation of law-abiding behaviour can be the result of a misunderstanding or of an unstated implication.

How is it possible that the way we organise our living together is irrelevant, that the content of the rules that govern it is indifferent, that measures providing for the death penalty or forbidding it, that forbidding some people what others are allowed to do, or banning discrimination, are equivalent and have the same dignity, because they organise our living together, thus making it possible?

It is evident that this is not the case.

But how can the law, as the complex of rules that regulate a society, be evaluated? What external element allows us to state that we agree with its content, or to establish whether a law is to be left as it is or changed, whether we have to respect it or break it?

4. 'Justice' is an Ambiguous Word

The value of laws was, and still is, assessed in relation to the notion of 'justice'.

Even this notion, however, turns out to be strongly ambiguous.

First of all, the term is employed with different meanings. It is used indifferently to refer to justice and to its administration.

The first meaning indicates a yardstick, a basic principle of living together, or an aspiration – something people aim at in their own interest or in their relationship with others. For this meaning we have a wealth of adjectives (social justice, distributive justice, retributive justice, and so on), all of which qualify the term giving it a particular meaning in relation to the field to which it is applied.

The second meaning of the term 'justice' describes a way of managing that eminently practical mechanism, namely the system humans have devised (although in very different ways) to solve controversies, to establish who is right and who is wrong in relationships between private parties (for instance, regarding the validity of a contract or a will), or between citizens and the public administration (for instance, to ascertain whether a license to build a house can be denied), or between the state and someone suspected of having committed a crime. When we talk about lawyers, judges, public prosecutors, court hearings, prisons, ministers, the lack of xerox machines, and so on, we use the term 'justice' in this second meaning.

When we say that justice is not functioning properly, we refer to its administration. On the contrary, when someone says that there is no justice in a certain country, they refer to the fundamental principles of living together. It is also said that laws (and/or behaviour) in a country are not in keeping with justice.

Even thus specified, this term is interpreted in very different ways.

Have you ever heard someone, apart from madmen and provocateurs, publicly declare that they pursue injustice?

Whatever the purpose, and regardless of the means used to achieve it, everybody describes themselves as a just person, as someone who aims to achieve justice.

In the name of this principle revolutions have broken out, uprisings have been stifled, genocides have been perpetrated, appalling crimes have been committed. How much evil has been caused under the banner of justice!

Whether it was earthly matters or religious questions, 'justice' was the word that authorised everything from the 'Holy Inquisition' (a practice whereby the Catholic Church tortured and burned alive thousands of people 'guilty' of heresy or witchcraft, and for which Pope John Paul II publicly asked forgiveness on 8 March 2000), to the Shoah (the Nazi extermination of millions of Jews, along with gypsies, homosexuals, disabled people, and regime opponents), down to the atomic bombs dropped on Hiroshima and Nagasaki (which, at the end of the Second World War, caused the death of hundreds of thousands of people in Japan).

Pope Lucius III certainly did not dedicate to injustice his decretal *Ad abolendam* which, in 1184, codified the condemnation of heretics. And in more recent times, Adolf Hitler, the Nazi dictator, made direct references to justice to legitimise his projects. To get an idea, you can read a couple of passages from his speech in Wilhelmshaven on 1 April 1939. "When other statesmen talk about the necessity of justice reigning in this world, then I may tell them that their crime is not justice, that their [Versailles] dictate was neither rightful nor legal, and that the permanent and vital rights of peoples come before this dictate. ... This Axis is the most natural political instrument in the world. It is a political combination of ideas which owes its existence not only to reason and the desire for justice, but also to strength inspired by idealism" [reproduced from *The British War Blue Book*]. Hitler certainly did not describe himself as a champion of injustice when he ordered the persecution and extermination of millions of people.

The same can be said of Stalin in the Soviet Union, of Pol Pot in Cambodia (they too had millions of human beings exterminated), and of who knows how many other perpetrators of genocides. Think of Chile's Augusto Pinochet, who overthrew Salvador Allende, bombing the government building and killing the legitimate representative of the country's institutions, or of Emilio Eduardo Massera and Jorge Rafael Videla who, in Argentina, organised a coup d'état and caused the disappearance of thousands of people suspected of holding opposing political views (many were thrown off high-flying planes). In his keynote speech of March 1976, Videla claimed that, "The respect of human rights does not come from the dictates of laws alone, or from international declarations, but is based on the deep, Christian belief that human dignity constitutes a fundamental right. We now take absolute powers to protect the natural rights of man – not to oppress liberty, but to exalt it, not to bend justice, but to establish it." Many other people have been responsible for the torture and violent elimination of dissidents, political adversaries, or simply people who were a nuisance to them. All these dictators represented their acts of bloody repression as a work of justice.

The different attitudes mentioned here are not necessarily displays of hypocrisy, deceit, superficiality, or ambiguity.

It must be remembered that there exist deep-ingrained, extremely different beliefs about what justice is.

Is it really possible, then, to define the deep meaning of the word 'justice' given this plurality of interpretations? If not a universal meaning (provided that there really is something that can be regarded as universal), at least the most shareable?

5.   Law Comes From God

The word 'justice' has always been taken as a point of reference to 'justify' the content of laws. This is not an easy task, given that the word 'justice' can refer to social systems (and hence sets of rules) that are clearly at odds.

The need to 'justify' law goes back to time immemorial.

At the dawn of human history there were no particular problems. Back then, law and justice coincided, because the former was thought to emanate directly from god. If god is just, and it is he who establishes the rules, then these cannot but be just. Later it was the priests who interpreted god's will and conveyed it to society, but the premise that justified the content of the norms was the same: law was an emanation of god; therefore laws continued to be just by definition.

A roughly similar approach continued to exist as long as it was believed that authority had a divine origin, as long as empires and absolute monarchs existed and succession was dynastic. As long as the Church had a secular role, anyone who held power (emperor, king, prince or pope) had a privileged relationship with god, deriving from Him his commanding power. As a consequence, the laws he enacted had a 'divine' justification. It is not an accident that even Napoleon Bonaparte, on 2 December 1804, crowned himself emperor in front of the pope, as the representative of god on earth, and the ceremony took place in Notre Dame Cathedral. According to this view, law was justified by its source.

On closer inspection, though, there was no certainty about the content of the term 'justice'. In effect, even god's word was not always unambiguous and, with a modicum of effort, one could search the Scriptures to find contradictory justifications for laws whose content was diametrically opposed.

Here are some examples of the, at least apparent, mutual incompatibility of god's words.

On the one hand, divine justice is intended as separation, exclusion, elimination, and spoliation:

Every morning I will put to silence all the wicked in the land; I will cut off every evildoer from the city of the Lord. (Psalm 101, 8)

My angel will go ahead of you and bring you into the land of the Amorites, Hittites, Perizzites, Canaanites, Hivites and Jebusites, and I will wipe them out. Do not bow down before their gods or worship them or follow their practices. You must demolish them and break their sacred stones to pieces. ... I will send my terror ahead of you and throw into confusion every nation you encounter. I will send the hornet ahead of you to drive the Hivites, Canaanites and Hittites. ... Little by little I will drive them out before you, until you have increased enough to take possession of the land. (Exodus, 23, 23-30)

For a fire will be kindled by wrath, one that burns down to the realm of the dead below. It will devour the earth and its harvests and set afire the foundations of the mountains. I will heap calamities on them and spend my arrows against them. I will send wasting famine against them, consuming pestilence and deadly plague; I will send against them the fangs of wild beasts, the venom of vipers that glide in the dust. In the street the sword will make them childless; in their home terror will reign. The young men and young women will perish, the infants and those with grey hair. (Deuteronomy 32, 22-25)

I will send four kinds of destroyers against them, declares the Lord, the sword to kill and the dogs to drag away and the birds and the wild animals to devour and destroy. I will make them abhorrent to all the kingdoms of the earth because of what Manasseh son of Hezekiah king of Judah did in Jerusalem. ... I will reach out and destroy you; I am tired of holding back. I will winnow them with a winnowing fork at the city gates of the land. I will bring bereavement and destruction of my people, for they have not changed their ways. I will make their widows more numerous than the sand of the sea. At midday, I will bring a destroyer against the mothers of their young men; suddenly I will bring down on them anguish and terror. The mother of seven will grow faint and breathe her last. Her sun will set when it is still day; she will be disgraced and humiliated. I will put the survivors to the sword before their enemies. (Jeremiah 15, 3-9)

On the other hand, in keeping with a conciliatory, friendly vision of justice, we also read:

> If you come across your enemy's ox or donkey wandering off, be sure to return it. ... Do not oppress a foreigner; you yourselves know how it feels to be foreigners, because you were foreigners in Egypt. (Exodus 23, 4, 9)
> Love your neighbour as yourself. (Leviticus 19, 18)
> This is what the Lord says: "Go down to the palace of the king of Judah and proclaim this message there: 'Hear the word of the Lord to you, king of Judah. ... This is what the Lord says: Do what is just and right. Rescue from the hand of the oppressor the one who has been robbed. Do no wrong or violence to the foreigner, the fatherless or the widow.' " (Jeremiah 22, 1-3)
> You have heard that it was said, 'Love your neighbour and hate your enemy'. But I tell you, love your enemies and pray for those who persecute you, that you may be children of your Father in heaven. He causes his sun to rise on the evil and the good, and sends rain on the righteous and the unrighteous. If you love those who love you, what reward will you get? Are not even the tax collectors doing that? And if you greet only your own people, what are you doing more than others? Do not even the pagans do that? Be perfect, therefore, as your heavenly Father is perfect. (Matthew 5, 43-48)

This contradiction was not viewed as upsetting: you could draw from the Word of God according to the needs of the moment, finding in it an alibi for even the most horrible brutality, or a motivation for brotherhood and solidarity.

6.   Law is Just If It is 'Natural'

The practice of justifying right with its divine origin still remains undisputed today in some parts of the world, and periodically reasserts itself in our own culture as well. (Just remember the Nazi's explicit appeal to their alleged closeness to god: '*Gott mit uns*', 'God is with us'.)

Parallel to this, however, as a more secular vision of society gained ground starting from ancient Greece, people stopped invoking god alone to justify the law, and a point of view developed in which the idea of 'naturalness' was central.

This idea was based upon the assumption that all human beings had an inborn, universally shared set of fundamental principles. In other words, it was thought that all people, no matter where they had been conceived or what situation they were put into, had an inner awareness that, in principle, killing is not good, getting possession of other people's things is not good, bearing false witness is not good, and so on.

Divine immanence, however, had not vanished. God was always in the background, functioning as the author of those 'natural' principles embedded in the heart of everyone. Yet he had, indeed, moved to the background, and his presence was not strictly necessary to justify law. It would have sufficed to regard those 'natural' principles no longer as having been implanted by god into the heart of every person in order to be able to do away with his presence when attempting to confer legitimacy on rules.

According to this line of thought, law is just inasmuch as its content coincides with these innate principles (called 'natural right' because they are seen as 'naturally' embedded in every person), and becomes all the more unjust as it moves further away from them.

But the passing of time, the evolution of society, and the discovery of other cultures and civilisations sowed doubts about this way of thinking too.

People gradually learned from concrete experience that not everybody in the world shares the same principles, that these can vary – sometimes greatly – from each other, and can even contradict one another.

Arguably, the only universal taboo in all cultures is incest. Accordingly, the only universal principle would be the ban on sexual intercourse between direct blood relations – which, by the way, in Italy is only punished in certain circumstances. All the rest varies, although in different ways and with different degrees of intensity.

It is not true that any individual bears engraved on his/her heart a rule which forbids killing, getting hold of other people's possessions, bearing false witness, and so on.

Therefore, the idea of legitimising rights on the basis of innate principles shared by all individuals progressively declined.

7.   Law is Just When It Exists

Given how difficult it is, not to say impossible, to find satisfy-ing parameters for verifying the justice or injustice of the law, it was thought adequate to evaluate it not on the basis of its content, but of the procedure followed to create it.

From this perspective, the law is not just because it coin-cides with god's word or because it translates into law the basic principles shared by all human beings. Law is just because it is issued by institutions that are in charge of doing so and the requisite procedures have been followed.

Thus, in a parliamentary democracy, a law is just when it is passed by parliament, after the bill has been proposed, debated, and approved by the required majority, enacted, and published on the registry in which laws are collected.

In short, law can be said to be 'just' when it is positive; that is, when it has been created and is observed.

Any command, prohibition, imposition, or discrimination can, according to this line of thought, become the content of law.

Justice, therefore, is no longer the motivation of law, but a consequence of it: the right thing is what the law declares to be right, whether or not it is consistent with principles (or motivations) external to the law itself. Justice therefore loses any claim to universality and, even from a theoretical standpoint, admits of the existence – or even coexistence – of several varieties of law, where each can be described as 'right' as long as it exists and is enforced in a certain territory.

8.   From Subject to Citizen

In relatively recent epochs in human history, the legitimacy acquired by law on the basis of its authorship and procedures went hand in hand with radical changes in the organisation of the state.

In the context of Enlightenment thought, around the mid-18th century, Charles-Louis de Secondat, Baron de La Brède et de Montesquieu, gave substance to an idea that was incubating at the time, and would later give rise to legality.

Previously, the monarch's power was truly absolute. The king was the owner of legislation, government, and justice: all powers were concentrated in his hands. He made laws, enforced them, and checked whether people's actions (including his own) were consistent with the norms he himself had introduced. The people who were ruled by him were completely at his mercy: they were subjects, and their relationships, possessions, and lives depended entirely on his unrestrained power. Except for the occasional instance that moved in the opposite direction – such as the *Magna charta libertatum*, which in 1215 restricted the power of the English monarch – this was the power structure which dominated most of humanity's history.

Enlightenment thought urged that the individual should be recognised as such, for the very fact that he or she exists. Such recognition implies that each person has to be protected against the interference of power, that he or she has to be granted freedom of movement and thought, and that his or her reasons can be accepted, even when they clash with the interests of power.

Montesquieu developed the organisational structure that would later allow subjects to become citizens. Namely, if power, now absolute and concentrated in the hands of one monarch, had been divided and shared among different institutions (in this case three: legislative, executive, and judicial, each having as their respective tasks to legislate, to govern, and to check whether laws are respected), each could have exercised only a part of it, and at the same time would perform a controlling and limiting function on the exercise of power by the other institutions, thus preventing possible excesses. Nobody would continue to be at the mercy of one single power manager, be it a person, an institution, or a faction of sorts. On the contrary, thanks to these very restrictions and to the control each power would exercise on the others, nobody would be at the mercy of anyone.

The separation of powers is a premise for the creation (and a pre-requisite for the preservation) of a society in which rights and duties are equally distributed, and therefore everybody has a comparable share of opportunities from and obligations towards society.

The principle was first shared by large sections of that part of the population that had the ability to give form to their views and make them known, and was then gradually applied. Parliamentary systems were introduced, and the making of laws was increasingly taken away from the monarch and handed over to a parliament.

When members of the legislative assembly began to be elected by citizens, rather than appointed by the monarch, when the selection of those holding the executive power went from the arbitrariness of a ruler to the decision of citizen representatives, it was noted that the legitimation of laws had its roots in the will of the people, who had chosen their spokespeople and given them access to parliament, and this choice in itself was an indicator of what the content of laws should have been according to their aspirations.

In some respects, it was a return to origins. At the dawn of human history, law was just because it came from god; in the new era, law was just because it came from the people, from the nation. In other words, the source continued to be the precondition for the acceptance of the norm.

Yet given that the individuals who make up the people, the nation, the citizenship, do not necessarily share the same views and do not enjoy the same standard of living (on the contrary, opinions can differ), it was agreed that the only legitimate maker of rules – who could enact laws – was the majority, the highest number of people who think the same about the same matter (or more commonly, about how to live together).

As was briefly mentioned, although it had emancipated the individual from the condition of being a subject, this new conception legitimised an extreme subjectivisation of the notion of justice itself, conferring 'dignity' upon attitudes formerly requiring an explanation and justification, the use of elaborate arguments to persuade someone of the 'rightfulness' of laws and of the view they rested upon.

The same force that led to freedom from absolute power, and to the secularisation of law (the separation from its fictitious link with god), had one further consequence - or collateral damage, as we would put it today – in its attempt at creating a society of equals. It justified any content of law expressed in the name of the majority.

Part II
Horizontal Society and Vertical Society

9.   The Vertical Society

Why can people, even in good faith, attribute such different, conflicting, or even contradictory, meanings to the term 'justice'? Why can this word turn out to be ambiguous?

In my view, this depends on the content it expresses.

And this content is in turn the product of differing, deep beliefs about human relationships. It is the product of the *weltanschauung*, or philosophical approach, as it were, that each person, perhaps unconsciously, has about the meaning of existence, about humankind and how it is supposed to evolve and progress, the optimist's or pessimist's view of it, and hence the value attributed to the individual.

Some people see humanity essentially as an animal species, governed by the same rules which regulate the development of other living species. They take an attitude of distrust towards the individual who is regarded as a non-individualised part of the mass, and is somewhat relegated to the background, slipping out of focus.

From this perspective, the progress of human beings takes place by selection. The strong, the cunning, the powerful, the 'fit', are selected 'naturally'. This gives dignity to their person, makes it deserving of consideration, and defines them as individuals. The weak, the different, those who lag behind, who do not fit properly into this design, get progressively eliminated.

The consequence of this deep belief is that the design whereby progress is achieved by discarding the unfit, must be supported. If nature puts living beings on a scale, if it leaves in the shadow those who cannot keep up, if it allows the elimination of those who hamper development, the task of human beings – who have acquired the ability to do so – is to contribute to that design.

Typical of this view is the idea that humanity is organised into a hierarchical scale: those who have no abilities must be discarded; those who are unfit should occupy the lowest steps, and progressively, the more qualities one possesses, the higher the level one is assigned to, right up to the top reserved for the chosen few, the best, the most cunning, the strongest, the fittest. And it often happens that all these qualities are attributed to one person, who is attributed the role of supreme chief – just like in animal communities. It is also typical of this particular way of thinking that those who belong to the top levels do not identify at all, or very little, with those who belong to the bottom levels.

On this view, individuals do not have a value in themselves: they acquire or lose importance depending on whether or not they fit into the evolution of the species.

Countless times in the course of history, subordination and discrimination have been justified on the grounds of the presumed inadequacy in certain individuals not able to be placed on the same level as the others, as in the case of women, slaves, blacks, or people belonging to certain ethnic groups.

A representative example is apartheid in South Africa, where, until the early 1990s, whites (who made up one fifth of the total population) occupied over 85% of the territory, owned 75% of the total income, and had an infant mortality rate ten times lower than that of the black population forced to live in ghetto cities and facing constant repression and discrimination.

In this vertical model of organizing society, there is an index which reveals how well each person fits in the evolution of the species, namely the level they occupy on the social scale. The higher individuals rank, the richer, the more powerful, famous, influential they are, the more they are the product of the evolution of the species, and the more instrumental they are in its further development. Conversely, the lower they rank, the poorer, the more powerless, unknown and uninfluential they are, the more their existence is unimportant, even sometimes harmful to the development of humankind.

From this point of view, a person is not an end; he or she does not have to be protected. Instead a person is liable to transform into an instrument for the advancement of the fittest, who are in turn destined to advance their species further, and can (but it would be more accurate to say 'should') be eliminated when they become useless or cause harm. Consequently, justice consists in promoting and preserving hierarchy, honouring privilege, and eliminating – sometimes physically – those who are harmful.

This was Hitler's view. For him, "Monkeys put to death any members of their community who show a desire to live apart. And what the apes do, men do, too, in their own manner," (*Hitlers Tischgespräche*) and "Nature ... begins by establishing life on this globe and then watches the free play of forces. Those who show the greatest courage and industry are the children nearest to her heart and they will be granted the sovereign right of existence over all the others, including the weak." (*Mein Kampf*).

Howsoever different, Lenin's ideas were the product of a similar view of the individual. He was quoted as saying, "It is true that liberty is precious; so precious that it must be carefully rationed." He claimed that "the replacement of the bourgeois state by the proletarian state is to take place through a violent revolution. The suppression of the proletarian state, namely the suppression of any state, is not possible except through an 'eradication' " even of the people who oppose it. In a subsequent stage, each attempt at escaping "this popular accounting and control will inevitably become so incredibly difficult, such a rare exception, and will probably be accompanied by such swift and severe punishment (for the armed workers are practical people ...), that the necessity of observing the simple, fundamental rules of all human community life will very soon become a habit" (*The State and Revolution*), clearly as a result of an imposition from the top. This attitude was just as pervasive, if not more pervasive, in the thought of Stalin, Mao, and of dictators in general.

In other cases in which, contrary to what happened in Nazi Germany and in the Soviet Union, selection is not imposed by dictatorship, it happens (to put it shortly) as a result of a certain idea of competition. As is well-known, to compete means to contend. A competition involves a winner and a loser. If this model is applied to personal relationships of whatever kind, the result is that you will relate to other people with the aim of winning (that is, defeating) in mind. In the field of ideas, commerce, and in the organisation of life together, selection takes place through competition: the winner climbs the ladder of social hierarchy; the loser slips down. When they get to the bottom, losers become useless and, if necessary, can be neutralised or eliminated – by segregation or physical elimination. The same happens to those who are a burden even prior to competition: the madman in the asylum, the deviant in prison.

This pyramidal organisation goes hand in hand with opacity and the poor circulation of information. The function of this opacity and lack of information is, on the one hand, to preserve the hierarchical structure. Those of a lower ranking, besides having few or no rights, also have little or no information, and no access to the inner workings of institutions. Hence they are unable to develop critical views based on documents, and are entirely dominated by a power whose actual size and nature is unknown. On the other hand, opacity and lack of information function as the precondition for climbing up the ladder of hierarchy, for instance by 'stepping on the toes' of someone who occupies the next higher level through a secretive management of information.

The organisational scheme of a vertical society is relatively simple because conflict situations are mostly solved by applying the principle of the hierarchical scale, where those who have a lower position always have to capitulate.

Despite this simplicity, the need for opacity and disinformation mentioned above favours the development of complex bureaucratic machines that dispense knowledge and responsibility.

The vertical model, then, applies not only to members of the same nation, but to entire populations.

The inhabitants of planet earth today have an almost endless history behind them. Its timeline can be traced back for millennia, and we can observe and identify the signs left along it by the cultures of past civilisations. Ever since the dawn of time, clashes between tribes, peoples, and nations have been solved through conflict, separation, submission, and elimination.

For individuals belonging to the same group, living together has mostly turned into 'dis-living', an existence informed by the principles of exclusion and separation. Neologisms aside, the cause of this may be that the belief in progress by separation was the dominant feeling, the guideline humans most consistently followed throughout their history.

This model was largely applied – and frequently continues to be applied – in relationships between individuals and between nations, through war, deportation, and genocide.

Ideas and beliefs of different natures have appeared several times throughout the history of humankind. Apart from a few exceptions, however, they have been cultivated and developed only in the sphere of religion (and have been aimed more at determining what classifies as moral behaviour rather than developing an actual discipline of social relations), or at least grounded the existence of assumed differences between individuals. The Athenian Republic, Aristotle (who claimed that the unjust man is he who does not observe equality, and that which is unjust is unequal), Socrates, Plato, all of whom are regarded as essential points of reference for a civilised, democratic notion of society, they too took for granted that humanity was divided into free people and slaves. For them, too, the basic principle coincided with separation and discrimination.

Apart from rare exceptions, societies were organised according to this hierarchical scheme until a very recent historical period, when the opposite view, that of a horizontal society, emerged strongly not just in collective conscience, but also in the discipline of human relations.

10. The Horizontal Society

There is another way of thinking about community, not based on hierarchy, but on the idea that humanity advances through a harmonious process in which the collaboration of everyone according to their abilities contributes to the liberty of individuals and the progress of society as a whole.

The founding element here is the very opposite of what leads to disproportion, separation, and exclusion. Humanity does not live, does not emancipate itself, does not progress by selection; rather it does so by paying attention to each of its members. The origin of this idea lies in the belief that all individuals are significant in themselves, that they embody a value, a dignity. This way of thinking is in turn the result of recognising in others the same 'nature' that everyone sees in himself or herself.

This recognition is not limited to the group you belong to: individuals do not only identify with themselves, their family, (some of their) classmates, supporters of the same football team, or with those who live in the same district, attend the same church, follow the same faith, have the same skin colour, speak the same language, or express the same ideas.

Recognising others - all others - has as an effect perceiving yourself as part of humankind (and not just of specific sections of humanity, like a family, a school, a fan group, a country, and so on) and the awareness of a connection, a common denominator with each of its members, namely the species.

The sense of belonging and identifying with others triggers discomfort by their problems and satisfaction at their well-being. All these feelings together form a texture which links anyone who participates in the social aggregation. It can be described as solidarity - if we take it to mean the awareness of belonging to a community and the willingness to offer and receive help in an attempt at better satisfying the needs of each member of the society.

In short, it is not unlike a family or (better still) a closely-knit group of friends, where mutual help, solidarity, and supporting each other in difficult times also extend to the other members of humankind. Of course the intensity of emotional bonds changes depending on how close the person is. Whereas everybody experiences great suffering when witnessing the unhappiness of someone close, feelings for unknown people are less intense and less lasting, but the feeling of being part of a whole is still there. Thus one may be hurt by the news of some distant population being crushed: the mutual massacres of the Tutsi and Hutu in Rwanda and Burundi in the recent past, the extermination of the desaparecidos some 15 years before in Argentina, the massacre in the Japanese cities of Hiroshima and Nagasaki caused by the atomic bomb at the end of the Second World War.

Every now and then we hear about people who dive into the stormy sea to save someone who is at risk of drowning, or who runs into a burning apartment to rescue someone trapped inside. Sometimes these actions cost the lives of those who attempt them. What drives these people into action is the recognition of the other as a fellow person, to the point that they can put their very lives at risk for them.

From this perspective, by the very fact that anyone exists, he or she constitutes an aim, an end, a dignity to protect. Therefore segregation becomes a contradiction, and can only be allowed in exceptional cases.

To think that humanity improves when each of its members improves, is not just a way of feeling, an underlying existential belief, but also a notion grounded in considerations of utility, which develops along two different lines.

The first aspect has to do with the observation that everybody can contribute in different degrees to the improvement of society. Therefore it is evident that, in the long run, the exclusion of 'different' people would only slow down, or even hinder, the harmonious development of the human species.

There are countless examples (not just in the field of art) of 'strange' people who sometimes have extremely troubled personal relationships, but whose irreplaceable contribution has enriched the heritage of humanity.

Vincent Van Gogh, who was marginalised in life and honoured after death, once burned his hand to prove his love to his cousin. He cut the lower part of his left ear, wrapped it, and took it to a brothel to give it to a prostitute of whom he had grown fond. He was hospitalised for mental illness several times, sometimes of his own free will, and put a bullet in his head at the age of 37. He is not an isolated case. Michelangelo Merisi, known as Caravaggio, was a violent, quarrelsome man, and spent part of his life on the run.

Should these examples appear inadequate because the people involved are artists (and everyone knows that the oddity of artists – being usually coupled with genius – is acceptable), then think about the Nazi period and the fate that awaited several extraordinary individuals, exceptionally learned people, who were killed in concentration camps because they were 'different', or who miraculously survived the atrocities (such as the mother of Mario Capecchi, a Nobel prize winner for medicine) and would certainly have died if Germany had not been defeated. Think about the great minds who were burnt at the stake by the Inquisition: not even someone like Galileo would have been spared if he had not abjured. Or think of, for instance, Archimedes of Syracuse or Antoine Lavoisier, who lost their lives in times of history when the individual had no value.

As regards the second aspect, if you look at the current stage of human evolution, it is evident that the increasing number of disadvantages already affecting, or liable to affect, anybody in the near future (the extreme poverty of a substantial part of humanity, whose very survival is at risk; the proliferation of weapons, conventional or not, which could destroy humanity; the gradual depletion of energy sources and environmental resources, which are soon estimated to become scarce even in the richer parts of the world) depends on the fact that the opposite development model is applied.

The organisational model of the horizontal society envisages an even distribution of responsibilities and opportunities, of duties and rights, and in particular the fundamental ones – those that constitute the basis of a decent existence and the precondition for the liberty of the individual. If, as we have seen, individuals are a dignity in and of themselves, if they are a value, the consequence of this is the right to life and to express one's opinion, to freedom of movement, to associate with others to pursue legitimate goals, to personal liberty, to have a home, to be given an education, to take care of one's health, and to find a job.

Since every person embodies dignity and value, these rights are granted to every member of society without exception. As a consequence, nobody can be physically eliminated, reduced to slavery, or prevented from expressing their opinion. At the same time, each member of society has the duty not to take another's life, to subjugate others to serve their own interests, to prevent others from speaking, and so on. This burden of duties is incumbent not only on individuals, but also on institutions, namely bodies that have been delegated a specific power in order to promote a more functional organisation of society. Thus a parliament, which has been delegated the task of making laws, has the duty not to interfere with the right to existence – by introducing, for instance, the death penalty. A mayor cannot refuse to issue a birth certificate that proves the identity of the person who is asking him for such a document. A head teacher cannot refuse to enrol in primary school a child who has turned six years old.

Naturally, living together may of course entail that a person's rights conflict with those of others. In a horizontal society, there is a guarantee of personal liberty, of the ability to move freely within the national territory, and to visit other countries. If, however, a person uses this freedom to damage others (for instance, someone is a killer for the mafia and travels to all corners of the country to murder people), then it is necessary to impose restrictions on this freedom of movement to render him harmless and thereby protect the rights of the other people. However, in order to prevent the possible transformation of a horizontal society into a vertical one (as we will see in the following chapters), limitations should be applied only for protecting other people's rights, without creating unjustified inequalities.

On the one hand, there are fundamental rights that are absolutely inviolable, since they cannot be separated from the recognition of individuals as values in and of themselves. Any limitation would run counter to this value. On this view, the death penalty and torture are to be avoided without exception. On the other hand, certain rights which are not strictly related to the dignity of the person can be subject to limitation, should these restrictions be necessary to protect fundamental rights of a higher order.

Duties, which mean restrictions and obligations, can only be imposed if their function is to protect other people's rights and the good functioning of social organisation. If each individual is entitled to the same rights and bound by the same duties, each person who participates in a society is effectively equal to the others before the law. Subjective peculiarities such as sex, ethnicity, religion, political ideas, and so on are completely irrelevant in this respect.

To say that 'we are all equal before the law' means to affirm that everyone in the same conditions must be treated in the same way. For instance, the possibility for an education must be guaranteed both for 'Aryan' and Jewish children, unlike what happened under the Fascist regime where the former were allowed to attend school and the latter were banned. It means that the violation of the right to life carries the same penalties whether the attacker is rich or poor, or belongs to one or the other social class – we should not forget that in the past, aristocrats and important people enjoyed privileged treatment. It means that if the top of society (the king, the president of the republic) and the less prominent fall ill, both of them must be treated. It means that Christians and Muslims can express their opinions in the same way, and it is forbidden to impose restrictions on communication that trench on the one but not on the other. For instance, both of them are to be granted the right to erect buildings consecrated to their own religion.

Equality before the law does not mean that the lives of all people have to be identical like photocopies, or that people are forced to lead a monotonous, repetitive existence. By guaranteeing on the one hand that fundamental rights (first and foremost the right to life) are recognised and on the other hand that all people are equal before the law, everyone is able to stay in control of their everyday life; to shape their future, and fulfil a free and decent life.

The horizontal type of society is not defined by the path traced by its members in the course of their lives, but by the guarantee that such path can be followed by everybody in non-discriminatory conditions, that is, conditions in which everyone has access to all possible tools.

In order to satisfy these needs, the horizontal society requires a complex organisation and various devices to allow it to develop and progress.

The existence of management positions, which do have powers from which others are excluded, is therefore necessary. Given the recognition of equality and fundamental rights, all citizens can aspire to these positions. They are carried out as a service to the community, not in the interest of individuals, political parties or religious faiths, friends, or powerful people.

Complexity, however, does not necessarily entail a huge and intricate administration consisting of a disproportionate number of bodies, each authorized to interfere with the lives of citizens. For rights to be really as such (not 'gracious concessions' from a power), the administration has to be streamlined and non-invasive, designed with only one aim in mind: to guarantee the pursuit of social goals, ultimately allowing all citizens to use society as a tool to satisfy their needs in the best possible way.

The horizontal model does not tolerate opaque institutions: the administration cannot but be transparent. It is necessary to verify its functioning and check whether everybody is actually treated in the same way, in all categories (hiring of personnel, supply of services, correctness of procedures, and so on). The horizontal society does not tolerate string-pulling, nor can it live with inadequate, biased, or incomplete information.

Since the horizontal society is based on the principle of equality, each of its members is entitled to a considerable range of choices, among them the designation of those who will be assigned the task of managing society. To be able to choose, you need to learn about the available alternatives. Information, therefore, is indispensable for the very existence of this type of society.

11.   Structure of the Two Models

The features of the one and the other type of society can, to some extent, blend with each other.

It may be that a society, on the whole, is organised vertically, but the horizontal system is also partly applied.

This has happened repeatedly throughout the history of humanity, for instance in countries which codified equality among citizens but at the same time practiced slavery. Classical Greece, in particular the Athenian Republic, is often taken as a model for a society which respected the individual. And yet it, too, acknowledged this disparity, the different consideration of human beings depending on the accidental circumstances they found themselves in, such as, for instance, the status of freeman or slave.

Today some democratic states apply the death penalty, which means that only within certain limits are individuals inviolable in their very existence. If these limits are transgressed, the principle of inviolability ceases to exist.

This mixed organisation can also be reflected in relationships between peoples. It may be, for example, that the stronger, better armed, richer nation regards only one part of humanity as worthy of respect, and sees another merely as an instrument, disposable, or exploitable depending on the situation. This has happened, for example, in a relatively recent era when the 'civilisations' of the Americas and Europe used to obtain slaves by (literally) stealing individuals from other populations.

The combination of these two conceptions of society and of the two corresponding organisational models generates a virtually infinite range of possibilities, the type of discipline of living life together, and hence the meaning of the word 'justice'.

12. Consequences of the Vertical Society

When the individual is seen as a mere instrument, when evolution obtains by rejecting the unfit, when relationships are based on a competition where the loser capitulates, then we are dealing with a vertical model of society whose founding values are separation and annihilation. Anyone who jeopardises individual interests, the goals, the privileges of an individual, a population, or a nation, is to be regarded as an enemy. They are other, different, and cannot be recognised as fellow human beings because the only recognisable fellow humans are the other members of the 'chosen' group (many think in terms of closeness to god), the only one that is permitted to advance.

States who embrace this social model do not adopt general measures to guarantee and protect what is necessary for individuals to create a basis for their existence, and to acquire the tools needed to advance (education, healthcare, labour).

The state, the community, does not offer services in these areas or, when they do, their quality is poor. An adequate education, one that allows citizens to find a decent job, is expensive – sometimes so expensive as to put literally a mortgage on the future of those who depend on it. If the family cannot or will not pay school fees, students take out loans which they have to repay at a future date. Therefore a good part of their future income will not be spent on basic needs, to purchase a house, or for personal expenses, but to pay back the loan. There are corrective measures, such as study grants for those who achieve brilliant results in education or sport, but for the masses, for those who do not excel, the bottom line is that a schooling which offers job prospects remains a privilege of the few.

The same happens with healthcare. In some countries, hospitalisation is dependent on owning a credit card or having substantial insurance. Those who do not possess these do not get treated at all, or can only be treated in charity facilities which are less efficient than paying hospitals. Lastly, where there is no labour security competition between workers is ruthless, and people can end up on the side of the road without justification.

Since, according to this approach, people who have caused damage to others must be neutralised, the most practical way to deal with offenders is their exclusion from the rest of society, either by prison segregation or by physical elimination (death penalty). In the People's Republic of China, capital punishment has killed thousands of people, while in the whole federation there are over two million prisoners (which makes you wonder whether prison is also used, maybe not entirely consciously, as a solution for unemployment).

As for attitudes towards other peoples, it is again vertical societies which admit and justify the practice of war. The way international disputes are settled is the result of the same fundamental idea that governs relationships among citizens within the state. The 'foreign' population is the other, different, unacknowledged, and can – or maybe must – be used like an instrument when it is useful, or annihilated when it causes injury. Hence the justification for colonial wars (whereby even nations regarded as sophisticated democracies took possession of boundless territories in continents where natural resources abounded), the wars of expansion which plagued Europe for long spells, and for the 'pre-emptive' wars of today.

When this principle is applied to a different ethnic group, it can justify the enslavement of black people, apartheid in South Africa, the Shoah in Germany (and to a certain extent also in Italy). When it is applied to the sexes, it leads to the marginalisation of women who are denied contact with the world outside their family and the right to vote.

War is often preceded by a process of true indoctrination, whereby the enemy acquires the traits of a monster.

The terrible abuses blacks were subjected to actually rested on the widespread belief that they were inferior beings. "[The British] have placed slaves on an equal footing with Christians, contrary to the laws of God and the natural distinctions of race and religion, so that it was intolerable for any decent Christian to bow down beneath such a yoke; wherefore we withdrew in order thus to preserve our doctrines in purity," wrote Anna Steenkamp in 1838 to explain the reasons for the Great Trek, the migration of Afrikaners to the inner territory of South Africa. And in 1883, A. B. Duprez wrote, "If we should disappear from South Africa, if we as a white people were to disappear, then we declare, in full consciousness to the whole world and in the name of the Afrikaner people, that we would rather die than accept integration and assimilation with the blacks." And as we go further back in history, it is worth remembering that it was debated in the past whether or not women had souls.

Since the social model is based on exclusion and neutralisation, its application in a vertical society requires substantial investment.

In order to defend territory within certain boundaries, people very soon began to enclose urban settlements with walls. It was often necessary to fend off attacks from people who did not recognise others as fellow human beings; other times refuges had to be built in order to avoid retaliation for aggressions which had been carried out. Today, walls thousands of miles long are designed to prevent the 'different' from emigrating without a permit to a country wealthier than their own.

In order to defend ourselves from the 'different' who live close to us and to neutralise criminals, we have built so many prisons that the total number of people incarcerated there equals the population of a city. The 'security' industry (including pre-emptive measures such as alarms, security companies, police force equipment) is doing especially well, but what really calls for a disproportionate quantity of resources are the tools designed for 'conflict resolution' between states, namely weapons.

So many weapons are spread across the globe that, if we divided their total offensive power by the number of inhabitants of the earth, each of us would have a pile of trinitrotoluene weighing several kilos on our heads, and we could still die from chemical and biological weapons – which still exist although international conventions require they be destroyed. Substantial parts of the world are scattered with mines and/ or unexploded cluster bombs ready to kill.

Treating individuals like instruments, failing to acknowledge their value, organising relationships hierarchically, all these mechanisms repeat themselves even more clearly when it comes to our environment, which is exploited beyond its capacity. This exploitation poses a serious threat to the future of the planet and of the next generations, who will increasingly experience a lack of the most basic elements of life, primarily water.

Another consequence of this conception is to regard as 'fair' the fact that the world is divided into well-off and disadvantaged areas.

On the other hand, it is obvious that some of the factors typical of the vertical society can be viewed positively. Its organisation is very simple. The general principles, that those above are right and those below are wrong, that whoever makes mistakes or does not fit into the scheme is to be removed or eliminated (or otherwise abandoned), and that society has no responsibility whatsoever towards individuals except to guarantee order, all these render its administration neither difficult nor complex.

The fact that this model was applied throughout most of humanity's history makes it look, at least superficially, like the 'natural' way for people to live together. Therefore no reflection, in depth-analyses, or cultural upheavals are needed to justify it.

Its philosophical roots, which harken back to the criteria of natural selection, are grounded in the assertion that, in a limited system, the unequal distribution of resources is necessary and inevitable because there would not be sufficient resources for all.

13. Consequences of the Horizontal Society

In the horizontal model, social and economic resources are employed to guarantee that every person is respected, and that their fundamental rights are protected. First of all are life, healthcare, education, housing, and work, and then, in logical order (but not in order of importance), freedom of self-determination and liberties pertaining to the expression of thought in all domains, including politics and religion.

Respecting the individual involves imposing some restrictions on the powers the state has over them. For instance, ruled out here is any institution terminating a member of the human race; similarly banned is any interference with the physical person of an individual.

Healthcare is generalised: everybody who wants it, is entitled to it, in particular those too who cannot afford it. Therefore substantial economic resources are earmarked for healthcare.

Special attention is given to the education of all people. Nobody can be discriminated against. On the contrary, everybody must be guaranteed a free, adequate education, irrespective of their disposable income. Therefore not only are considerable resources earmarked for schooling, but teachers and workers are selected on the basis of their abilities and have access to continuing education. Their work is acknowledged in terms of both social dignity and remuneration.

The efforts of society are directed towards assuring that each member can live in a decent house and find a stable job which suits their abilities, and from which they cannot be removed without justification. Occasional unemployment does not bar rights to financial means guaranteeing a decent life.

As for attitudes towards other peoples, when there is a deep belief that each person has value and dignity, relationships are based on the recognition of the other. There is a tendency towards welcoming and integrating, rather than separating and rejecting.

The basic principle of value and dignity of the individual excludes the physical elimination of others, who are not 'foreigners' but fellow human beings. They are, again, individuals. They are not identified as enemies because they live elsewhere, follow a different culture, or have a different skin colour and a different (or no) religion. Otherness is not a threat to security.

Within this framework, weapons can only be used to defend oneself from attack by those who persist in organising themselves vertically, believing in the advancement by selection, separation, and annihilation of the different. In this way, financial resources can be channelled into the development for disadvantaged populations and recognition of the dignity of all their members. This goal is not achieved by promoting charitable intervention, but by providing the tools (knowledge first of all, that is, education) which can help all human beings plan their own future.

From the respect of individuals follows respect for the environment, for natural resources, for their ultimate use and renewability.

The list of objections that can be raised against this social model is quite long.

One objection may be that the horizontal society is anti-historical and anthropologically unfeasible because, in the first place, it has apparently never been realised in its purest form: society has evolved through vertical, or at least mixed, systems. In the second place, it is undeniable that human nature is characterised by a strong aggressive drive and by a tendency to exploitation. Over time, these features would irreparably turn any horizontal society into a vertical one.

Another objection might be that societies tend to preserve the status quo rather than to promote progress. On this approach, inequality would actually be the break with tradition, pushing towards new balances and new rules, which would have to be broken again in order to attain further progress.

A further objection could be that a horizontal society flattens out everything and everybody, making life boring, taking away the drive towards diversity, and reducing incentives to behave properly, namely the acknowledgement and social advancement of individuals based on their merits (and any downgrading because of their faults).

A fourth objection could be that this model cannot be applied globally because natural resources are insufficient for satisfying the needs of all, and therefore selection is mandatory. Such a model is unmanageable, and hence unreal and utopian, for the very reason that it is applied to society in general. If all individuals constitute an irrepressible value and dignity, how do we solve the controversies in which the dignity of one individual clashes against that of another? For instance, if somebody tries to kill me, can the state take steps against that person which are at odds with the acknowledgement of his value as a person? Can they be imprisoned to avoid their reaching the goal of killing me? And if this is the case, would it not result in a limitation of one of their fundamental rights – personal liberty – and hence a denial of their value?

Actually, each of these objections can be easily answered. Only the last one requires a more complex reply.

The point of view of the first observation is not correct. The history of humanity is reduced to a static condition which has not undergone substantial change. Therefore no improvement is to be expected. It is probably correct to say that a horizontal society has never been achieved, but this does not rule out the possibility that humans can get progressively closer to it. We can think back to that moment (which varies from place to place) in the evolution of human society when human sacrifice was still a common practice. If we do not want to stray too far from our own culture, we can think of Agamemnon, who was willing to sacrifice his daughter Iphigenia to appease the anger of the goddess Artemis on the eve of departure for Troy. In those times, human sacrifices were an accepted practice and nobody could predict that they would be banned in the future.

We can go back to the dawn of Christianity, when slavery was so deeply rooted in the tradition of that epoch that even Paul, in his letters to the Ephesians and Galatians, accepted it and limited himself merely to urging a change in the relationship between a master and the slave – who, however, still remained a slave. Who could have predicted the abolition of slavery about 18 centuries later? Nobody, of course, because slave status was part of the culture at that time.

In the era of the Holy Inquisition, when torture was a widely employed method, not just for interrogation and cross-examination but as a punishment for the crime that had been committed, who would have even thought – with a modicum of verisimilitude – that, after the Enlightenment and Cesare Beccaria, torture would be, at least formally, abolished as a punishment, and only occasionally reinstituted – but in general censured – as a method to acquire information?

Today human sacrifices, slavery, and torture are banned, but the mere idea of eliminating them would have been unthinkable in times when they were an integral part of mass culture.

Those who do not have a dynamic view of history claim that we must continue to live with the mafia (they do not even imagine that the mafia culture can be defeated), and they have absolutely no ability to envision a model of social association different from the one that has been widely applied until now.

If we look at history dynamically, observing the progressive decrease in the level of human aggressiveness, nobody can rule out that violence may be, if not eliminated, at least contained; whereas from the static point of view of today, any prediction about the minimisation of violence turns out to be unreliable.

Is the horizontal society conservative? In some respects it is: it preserves by not eliminating, not destroying. It preserves the person. It preserves the environment, fighting as best it can any hastening of the end of our planet, and of our life possibilities. It opposes what is commonly referred to as 'sustainable development', because it is based on consumption and depletion of existing resources.

In other respects the horizontal society is proactive, and in a sense revolutionary for today, in a world where a substantial part of the population lives in poverty, where about one in five inhabitants of the planet does not have access to drinking water, and where the consumption of natural resources is increasing almost exponentially and yet people do not care about exhausting them or about environmental pollution; a world where it is clear that not everybody is guaranteed the most basic rights, such as the right to exist, and where the scope of their protection is bound to shrink.

A model whose application would overturn the existing situation would be profoundly innovative. It would carefully evaluate the costs and benefits of deploying particularly invasive technologies, checking case by case whether the greatest possible speed of transportation is really worth the investments it requires or is rather a way to satisfy an anti-economical fetish.

What is conservative, or rather restorative of a past that wreaked so much havoc, is actually the vertical model – the old model – one which does not envisage any novation and returns individuals back to the supremacy of their most instinctive part and to the degradation of reason.

The idea that the horizontal society flattens out the life of everyone, turning it into a carbon copy of everyone else's, is based on a misunderstanding. Equality before the law does not exclude diversity. On the contrary. Equality before the law, coupled with the recognition and protection of the fundamental rights of individuals, ensures that each person has the ability to create the life he or she is willing to undertake.

The horizontal society guarantees the basis, the point of departure, from which individuals can develop their own existence, and makes sure that the core of this foundation, namely personal liberty (both physical and mental), freedom of choice, education, health, and occupation, is preserved as far as possible.

Given these guarantees, everyone is indeed free to shape their own future in one way or another. Nobody is forced to climb the social ladder to acquire or preserve this freedom.

As for the objection based on the alleged scarcity of resources, one can reply that they appear to be scarce precisely because they are wasted and badly distributed, and because a substantial part of them is diverted from uses that are beneficial to the common good, and is instead employed for the production of weapons.

The objection that it would be impossible to organise a society unless one would consent, at least occasionally, to a violation of the fundamental rights of the individual, seems to be the one that gets closest to the heart of the problem. In order to analyse it, we need to tackle a series of preliminary issues – addressed in the following chapters – about fundamental rights and sanctions for violations, as given in the two social models.

14. Fundamental Rights According to the Two Models

In a vertical society all rights are dependent on an external variable, except for (but not always) those granted to the people at the head of the group. Since individuals are instruments, any of their prerogatives depends on the attainment of the end to which they are a means.

In Imperial Rome it was up to a father to decide whether a newborn baby was allowed to survive. This decision depended on his interests, beliefs, and feelings. In the Middle Ages, the existence of an individual depended – and still depends in some states – on whether he or she had committed a crime punished by the death penalty. In classical Greece, the personal liberty of an enemy depended on whether he or she was caught and reduced to slavery.

In a vertical society, restrictions on the right to life or to freedom are absolute. It depends on the fact that what has to be protected is first of all the type of organisation itself, in which the individual, regarded as an instrument, surrenders to the privileged few at the top of the social hierarchy. The hierarchy, in turn, is intrusive to the point of depriving subordinate individuals of their decision-making ability, which then gets replaced by that of the system. Thus, to name just one example, in some states the private expression of homosexuality is prohibited – which is tantamount to denying the right to free self-determination, even when the freedom of others is not threatened, because the hierarchy imposes a standard of 'justice' that disregards respect for the individual.

In a horizontal society too, there are limits to some rights. But when there is a limit, it is always set for reasons of functionality and reciprocity.

First of all, there are no limits to the right to life as long as one is a 'person'. The state, the institutions, cannot deprive a person of their life. Even when there are situations in which it is impossible to avoid taking a life (for instance, to free a hostage who would otherwise be killed, or in the case of defending against aggression), there is no such thing as the right to kill. In such situations killing is regarded as inevitable in order not to lose another life – that of the person who did not assault anyone. The loss of the perpetrator's, however, can only be justified (but not the act, which continues to be censured) if there was no alternative to the killing in that specific case. The life of anyone, including that of the aggressor, continues to have value, and the fact that they have been deprived of it is inevitable – but not just.

The same principle legitimates taking another person's life, whether or not there is an aggressor, when this is necessary to save one's own – always, and only, when there is no alternative.

Because the acceptance or rejection of the value of individuals is the premise of the horizontal society, the protection of their existence should never be put into question. But when can the existence of a person be defined as such? The issue is clearly a sensitive and complex one, and takes different shapes in a life's two book-end moments of birth and death.

In my view, it is difficult to deny that a fertilised egg is not yet a person, just as it is difficult to disprove that a fetus capable of autonomous life already is a person.

Just as clear is the fact that the decision to put an end to one's life is an expression of the right to self-determination, the right to decide for yourself what to do with your life. The focus of the horizontal society is not 'life', but the 'person', the individual. Forcing someone to live when they are not able to make a conscious choice to terminate their own existence is the expression of a hierarchical structuring of values, for the achievement of which the person remains an instrument.

In a horizontal society, this problem turns into a question of defining the limits of what is a legitimate intervention by someone in our life – by a woman for the fetus, by a doctor for the patient. It is a matter of identifying the terms within which the protection of individuals is to be effected without resorting to, for instance, short forms that lead in the opposite direction: life is sacred; suffering redeems, or, even, disabled, sick people, and anyone who is a burden to themselves and others has to be eliminated. These ideas reinstate an instrumental view of the individual.

In a truly horizontal society there can be no limits to the rights that protect the integrity and growth of the person, namely education, health, housing, and labour.

There is no transcending 'order' to be preserved; no hierarchies or privileges to be respected. Each person is equal to all others, and limitations to the rights of each individual are only justified in cases when their lack would compromise a higher right of the other. And any limitation always has to be reciprocal.

From this perspective, the nature of a social system can be tested by verifying the interchangeability of positions. If, by putting a person in the place of another, the set of fundamental rights they are entitled to does not change, then the society is organised horizontally. If the opposite is true, then the structure is vertical.

15. Sanctions According to the Vertical Model

To test the concrete practicability of a horizontal social system (and to answer the last objection mentioned in the previous chapter), one needs to reflect upon the consequences of the failure to respect rules.

Can a society which does not accept any kind of violation of fundamental personal rights (not even when it is committed by institutions to 'restore law and order') really guarantee respect for rules? What other measures could be adopted to prevent offences? How can the exercise of everyone's fundamental rights be protected without betraying the basic principle of the horizontal society – inclusion – which is incompatible with separation, exclusion, and elimination; that is, with the measures generally taken to neutralise those who infringe rights?

In a vertical society, where rights and duties, responsibilities and opportunities are unequally distributed, it is difficult to prevent those who have a heavy burden of duties and yet enjoy only limited rights, from committing offences. Thus one resorts to sanctions to contain noncompliance following the rather simple paradigm: if you violate a rule, I will inflict pain on you; this will deter not just you from violating the rule, but also those who see the pain inflicted upon you.

When the protecting of the excess of goods enjoyed by the top sectors of a society, big landowners for instance, is regarded as more important than ensuring that its base has an adequate means of livelihood (according to the estimates of the World Bank, in 2001, 1.2 billion people were living below the poverty line), it is very hard to keep 'the poor' from committing thefts, dealing in small quantities of illegal drugs, or resorting to prostitution or petty corruption, save by setting out and applying a penalty which intimidates – incarceration namely.

Respect for law (legality) is therefore guaranteed by means of threats and, in case of transgression, by inflicting punishment. In order to be effective this punishment has to represent for potential offenders a penalty worse than what they would face if they did not break the rule. The sanction must therefore consist of an evil, and the evil should in turn, at least in principle, follow a hierarchical scale so that its intensity matches the seriousness of the offence.

The Italian word '*pena*' (which can mean 'punishment', but also 'suffering') aptly expresses the idea that the penalty for those who infringe someone else's rights should first of all be suffering. The evil caused by violating rules is to be repaid with the evil inflicted by the punishment.

In this case we are dealing with the retributive function of punishment, a notion which in Western culture finds ideological, as well as historical, justification in the Biblical rule 'an eye for an eye, a tooth for a tooth': "If you gouge my eye out, I have the right to gouge out yours; if you break my tooth, I have the right to break your tooth." The expression, however, is isolated from its context, where it actually has a different meaning. Its original function was to set limits to the unconditional, boundless right of victims to take their revenge on those who had caused offence, and constituted progress compared to the previous era in which (using a similar example) the loss of an eye entitled the victim to take any type of revenge, including murder.

Because the punishment must consist of suffering and be proportional to the crime committed, in the 13th century for example (the time of Dante Alighieri, who, in his Divine Comedy, chose punishments inflicted on the damned according to the criteria of likeness to, or contrast with, the crime committed, thus highlighting the correspondence between sin and sentence), it sometimes happened that a thief was punished by having his hand cut off, because it was the hands being used to steal; or a perjurer would have his tongue torn out, because it was with his tongue that he had given false evidence; or someone who had joined a riot would have his foot cut off, because it was the feet which had allowed him to move and struggle. And in order to keep some proportion between the crime committed and the harshness of the punishment, the perpetrators of the most serious crimes were killed by inflicting upon them the most painful tortures.

The suffering-oriented and retributive nature to a criminal sentence is a constant in the vertical society, where detention is by far the most frequent consequence of violating fundamental rules. The duration of confinement is largely determined by the seriousness of the violation itself.

Because such a society is hierarchically structured, however, the closer one gets to the top, the more easily one can avoid punishment in practice, through (sometimes unnoticed) subterfuges of judges, or less harsh sanctions for offences that are typical for those at the top, or even immunity, all of which means that punishment is generally reserved for the lowest and bottom categories of the social pyramid.

There is no doubt that the death penalty is the product of the vertical society. Physical elimination tramples on the most basic of rights, the right to life.

The cultural link that connects prison and vertical society is just as clear. Imprisonment indeed means exclusion and separation, and is often in conflict with the rehabilitation into society of those who have broken rules. Those who have been incarcerated, save in a limited number of exceptions, continue to be excluded from the community even after regaining their freedom.

Given that the function of a sentence is to uphold the hierarchical order, the motives which led to the violation of the norm and the subjective or social conditions of those who have violated it are not particularly relevant. For example, it does not matter whether a crime was committed to meet survival needs or merely out of spite, and no relevance is attributed to the seriousness of the offence – which could even turn out to be negligible – or of the damage caused. These variables can affect the duration of the sentence, although in general they have no bearing on the nature of the sanction.

Since the underlying belief is that evil has to be repaid with evil, the effectiveness of the sanction at preventing future criminal behaviour becomes secondary, sometimes even irrelevant. That imprisonment does not achieve the aim of avoiding or reducing repeat offences is ultimately unimportant (in Italy, for example, two out of three people who come out of jail commit new crimes). Likewise no importance is given to the fact that, from an economic point of view, the cost of imprisonment is particularly high (again in Italy, it has been estimated at almost 150 euro a day for each convict).

For some people, prison becomes a real school of crime. When individuals are not particularly resistant to criminal behaviour (resoluteness which even people who have committed crimes can have), when they do not have a strong, deep-seated tendency to integrate back into the social fabric, imprisonment offers an encouragement to refine techniques for carrying out crimes and, above all, triggers a psychological process whereby convicts whose endeavours are most notorious become role models especially for young people. The tendency to emulate originates in the desire to climb the social hierarchy of deviancy, thus gaining prestige, respect, and power.

The reason why the vertical society is ready to pay such a high price is evident: seen from this angle, the consequence of breaking a rule is itself a selection criterion in the process of excluding, marginalising, and separating. Punishment is instrumental to the hierarchical organisation of society because it divides, draws a line between those who must have freedom and the others who must be discarded.

This is crystal clear if we think of the death penalty, which paradoxically is the most effective penalty because it makes that elimination final, preventing those who have broken the order from doing it a second time.

The function of prison, however, is more complex. Detention, if temporary, does not necessarily exclude future attacks on the social system; does not stop new offences from being carried out. But it somehow certifies, prolongs, and guarantees the layered structure of society. When this is deemed insufficient, detention is turned into a life sentence. Prison can be the point-of-no-return even when the crimes committed are not particularly serious. For instance, in some US states a rule was introduced whereby after a certain number of offences, regardless of how serious the crimes were, the offender never leaves prison again, and is forever excluded from society.

16. The Consequences to Offences in the Horizontal Society

The founding principle of the horizontal society has very different repercussions on the failure to observe rules.

As we have seen, the death penalty is absolutely incompatible with this organisation model. But prison, too, is not consistent with the principles of the horizontal society.

Prison compresses personal liberty (the freedom of movement, to nurture relationships with loved ones, to have contact with other people, to choose a real job, and so on) almost to the point of annihilating it and, in general, leads to the brutalisation of those who are confined there. Prison is the expression of a retributive, suffering-oriented view of punishment, one which clashes with a recognition of the individual's dignity. It constitutes an obstacle to the reintegration of convicts into society, and therefore to their ability to resume contributing towards harmonious communal life. Finally, prison does not achieve the ends it is used for: except for preventing those who are jailed from committing crimes (and only during their detention), it does not perform a specific preventive function, in that it does not contribute to preventing recidivism. Nor does it fulfil a general preventive function. In fact most of the time the threat of incarceration is not a deterrent to breaking rules. And, as we have seen, it is financially very expensive for a community.

Although the incompatibility between the horizontal model and prison (as exclusion and infliction of suffering) is plain to see, it seldom happens that a society, even when it is founded on the value and dignity of the individual, avoids choosing detention as a penalty for the breach of an almost unlimited number of rules. And it is just as rare that even those upholding the respect for the human person question the prison system and punishment in the literal meaning of the word. I speak from direct experience: apart from people who work in the field (quite a few actually), occasional enlightened minds, and some religious people, once you scratch the surface the belief emerges that prison, as it is now, cannot be done away with.

In my opinion, this depends above all on the deep roots of traditional culture in this particular area and, again, from the inability to see the history of humankind in its dynamic evolution.

Except for rare, limited periods of time, a penalty has always been identified with punishment. Indeed, punishment in the past used to be far more grievous and cruel than mere imprisonment. Until not so long ago in history, jails were just waiting rooms, where the prisoner would stay until the sentence was executed. It was a sort of pre-trial custody, to prevent those who were accused from evading their trial and those who had been convicted from evading execution of their sentence (which, more often than not, was death by terrible torture). For instance, Galeazzo Visconti, lord of Milan during the second half of the 14th century, devised a system for people sentenced to the capital punishment which led to their death after 41 days of torture (including the tearing off of the soles of their feet, the cutting off of hands, feet, and testicles), culminating in being broken by the wheel.

Prison, therefore, is an improvement on the punishments that were inflicted before it became the main solution for society's punitive needs, but its function is based on the same mechanism behind those previous penalties.

The reasons leading to imprisonment becoming the prime answer to a violation of law include not only the traditional equivalence between sanction on the one hand, and exclusion and suffering on the other.

The Church made no small contribution to consolidate this cultural model too. Forgiveness, the foundation of all

Christian thought – at least until the Reformation, was often relegated to the sphere of the individual's intimate relationship with God, and had no influence on the relationship between individuals, or between individuals and an authority. In the sphere of human relationships, separation and exclusion have prevailed (the so called 'list of banned books', which existed from 1559 to 1965 and excommunication are two examples of this attitude), a confusion between the concepts of crime and sin reduced a person to a tool in the struggle against evil, ultimately degrading the individual to the status of an object which could be dealt with in any possible way. And whether this treatment was aimed at some form of redemption after death had no bearing on the content of earthly relationships.

The notion that suffering is a source of salvation, even when it is imposed and not accepted, has contributed to reinforcing and spreading the culture of retributive punishment.

Additionally, the acceptance of prison is also connected with a cultural factor that has to do with the perception of security.

What protects us more from the evil wolf that wants to eat us (apart from killing it) than locking him in a cage? Thus we put those who have broken rules behind bars. And because these people are evil just like the wolf (but unlike it, they possess reason), we need to make them feel not only that crime does not pay, but that it even makes you suffer.

This being the common way of thinking, people do not realise – or refuse to believe – that there can be alternatives. But before Copernicus, too, nobody ever imagined that it could be the Earth revolving around the Sun, and not vice versa.

Resistance to considering the question of the consequences to rule-breaking within a perspective that is coherent with the root principle of the horizontal society is an indicator of the widespread inability to grasp the fundamental difference between the two organisational systems. In the horizontal social model, the purpose of justice is not to punish, but to repair and reconcile.

In the vertical model punishment, and hence the repression of crime, are fairly important matters for evident reasons having to do with the protection of the organisation system, where inequalities, privileges, and discrimination are inherent in the system itself. But in the horizontal society the process of establishing responsibility focuses less on the criminal trial. And therefore sanction is less important.

Because relationships do not centre on obedience, but on confrontation and dialogue, responsibility matters first and foremost in personal relationships: individuals are responsible for their actions and behaviours towards the people they are relating to. Responsibility also expresses itself in the political, professional, civil, and administrative sectors more strongly than in a vertical society.

Actually, responsibility first manifests itself as responsibility towards oneself. Because culture is based on a respect for others, individuals feel the need to check whether their behaviour is consistent with the model they rely on. Therefore in a horizontal society criminal law (supposing it should continue to be called such) is far less extensive, and only addresses that conduct which actually threatens the fundamental rights of people and their harmonious co-existence.

If a society is truly organised horizontally, then the incentives and occasions to break the law are far more limited. Of course, violations do not disappear. Given that human nature is a mix of instinct and reason, good and evil, impulse and reflection, self-centeredness and love, there will always be someone who breaks the law. But offences will be much less frequent than in a situation where the fundamental rights of every single person are not recognised.

The protection of basic rights indeed leads to a considerable decrease in incentives to offend, due not so much to a decrease in the need to resort to crime to satisfy basic necessities, but rather to the fact that the points of reference are different from those of the vertical society. When a culture is shaped by respect for the individual, when people recognise themselves in the other, when there is a widespread belief that the other has value and dignity, and at the same time rules are the practical, concrete application of that culture, then incentives to break the law are bound to remain marginal because most of the time the fact of sharing common rules makes the imposition of an obligation or prohibition unnecessary.

In the horizontal society therefore, deviance is less widespread. It is more of a pathological than a physiological condition – contrary to what occurs today in Italy where entire regions are governed more extensively by criminal powers than by legitimate institutions.

There will always be husbands who kill their wives out of jealousy, or mothers who kill themselves and their child in a bout of depression, or children who murder their parents to inherit the estate. There will always be someone who resorts to robbery to gain more money, but they will be exceptional, pathological cases. And pathology can be treated as a marginal phenomenon.

Because the main obstacle to deviance lies in the way of thinking, namely culture, violations are met with the disapproval of the community, and this disapproval is to some degree acceptable even to those who have broken the rule. (This happens much more rarely in a vertical society, where the room for self-justification is very broad, for reasons that have to do with culture and inequality.) And such violations are not physiological nor particularly frequent.

In the horizontal society, the purpose of criminal law (but it would be better to describe it as 'sanctions law') is to guarantee the fundamental rights of everybody, and their equality before the law. This, however, does not reflect the current trend in most Northern/Western cultures, where most transgressive behaviours are penalised (that is, punished as a consequence of the violation of laws), and where therefore the application of prison sentences is extended indefinitely.

All offences are not all equal. If we focus our attention on those which are today punished by incarceration, we will notice remarkable differences between one and another. Rule-breaking can be caused by passion, impulse, or by cold calculation. It can be occasional or part of a plan. It can threaten the integrity, physical or psychological, of an individual, or of property. It can attack individual or common possessions. It can cause irreparable, considerable, minimal, or trivial injury, and so on. Each offence ought to be met with adequate measures.

And it should not be forgotten that, in establishing the consequence of each violation, one should take into account the specific characteristics of the perpetrator and the type of crime committed. Would it not be more appropriate, for example, for someone who has run over a person, in addition to being disqualified from driving for a long period of time, to be obliged to offer assistance for a series of weekends in a hospital where victims of road accidents receive emergency treatment, rather than be threatened with imprisonment?

Would it not be more productive to oblige someone who has built a structure which does not comply with environmental protection standards, the rights of other people, or the security of those who will live inside it, not just to tear down the building, but to restore land to its previous condition (before the construction work made a mess of it), and to complete this action by paying some compensation to citizens for the inconvenience they have been put through?

By determining the most appropriate answer on a case-by-case basis, and keeping in mind the aim of rehabilitating the individual into society, we would be left with only a limited number of cases in which we need to resort to detention facilities, namely when this becomes necessary to prevent the same person from committing further infractions. In other words, prison would only be taken into consideration when it becomes impossible to obtain the same result through other means.

Except for those cases, all the remaining issues are to be addressed with other measures. In order to identify these, one needs first of all to make a distinction between the position of the victim and that of the perpetrator.

17.   Victim and Offender

How can a victim be compensated, how can the situation be repaired? In most cases, victims are satisfied with the restoration of the situation that existed prior to the offence, compensation for the distress they have suffered, and the recognition of the fact that their rights have been violated. Those who have their cars stolen are satisfied (compensated) with its retrieval, reimbursement for any damage to the vehicle, the recognition of the inconvenience caused by being deprived of it, and the community's acceptance of their reasons. Those who are defamed in a newspaper or on television are satisfied if their reputation is restored by a retraction, if they receive compensation for the distress resulting from having been maligned, and if they receive an apology. There are countless similar situations in which the victims can be compensated in similar ways.

But there are other offences whose consequences cannot be eliminated – or at least not completely – by subsequent restitutive behaviour. Those with a limb amputated, those subjected to torture, the parents of a child killed in a road accident, a sexually-assaulted woman, the survivors of a murdered person: how can they be compensated? It is evident in these cases that what is lost cannot be recuperated: the loss of a limb, of physical integrity, of a relative cannot be made up for. The value lost, however, can be restored or the irretrievable loss can be compensated for to some extent. Different methods have been experimented with, and have often yielded positive results.

In South Africa, the Truth and Reconciliation Committee managed to bring back peace to a country that went from the dictatorship of a white minority over a black majority, to apartheid, to democracy. The atrocities committed by whites to keep citizens of colour segregated often included torture and murder. One would have expected the outbreak of civil war, but this was avoided precisely because the Commission was able to initiate a process whereby victims and torturers eventually reconciled.

The Commission was formed as a consequence of recognising that (as Archbishop Desmond Tutu declared in an interview some years ago) if a mechanism had not been devised to cope with the injustices of the past, those very injustices would have continued to plague the new government, threatening the fragile structure of the young democracy.

The Commission was a place where, again in the words of Tutu, both victims and perpetrators had the opportunity to face each other as human beings. Some of them had the merit of recognising our common vulnerability as human creatures and, in that context, giving and receiving forgiveness. In order to achieve this, Tutu continued, first and foremost you have to recognise that your behaviour was wrong, admit your responsibility, and apologise to those who have been damaged by this wrongful behaviour. The genuineness of repentance must be demonstrated by the form of reparation.

What is restored to the victims in these cases; how are they compensated for the losses they have suffered? The victims receive information about what really happened. They acquire 'the truth' and obtain the consideration of the community they live in, regaining their dignity as individuals. They receive the culprit's confession, that is, the admission that the latter was the wrongful cause of the victim's pain. The wound suffered gets repaired – insofar as is possible.

The bottom line is that a conversation, a face-to-face meeting, between victims and perpetrators (in the presence of those who can facilitate this process) leads to reparation, and forms the basis for similar procedures not necessarily related to such epoch-defining issues as the end of apartheid in South Africa, but which still often yield satisfying results. These methods have been adopted in several countries, among them

Australia, the US, Canada, France, Germany, Austria, Belgium, and Italy as well, especially for juvenile crime.

To have a general idea of how this mechanism works, we can describe briefly the procedure applied regarding juvenile offenders in Australia. The police moderate the meeting where the participants include the person responsible for the harmful behaviour, the victim, the victim's family, and members of the communities in which the parties live. The victim is encouraged to participate first. The offender describes how the events took place. Once all participants have discussed the case, the victim proposes the content of reparation, and if the request is accepted, a reparation agreement is drawn up.

This process serves to restore dignity to the victim and repair the damage suffered. But at the same time it aims at rehabilitating the offender so as to return to society, evoking hence feelings of shame that can help make reintegration possible. It is a process which helps the acceptance of responsibility through knowledge (of the facts and of the victim).

Reconcile, repair, mediate, reintegrate, all these words describe the process of reconstructing what was broken, mending the social fabric torn thus by the offence. If this operation is successful, its effect is preventive both in the specific case (if the offender is successfully reintegrated into society it is unlikely that he or she will turn away again from it), and on a general level (the draw of living together in harmony minimises a tendency for deviance; general reproach and personal shame are a deterrent against breaking the law). This method is far more effective than prison, which has turned out to be a school of crime and a breeding ground for repeat offenders.

Clearly, in the case of particularly serious injury, complementary measures are necessary, usually healthcare and psychological counselling, which can help victims get over the trauma they experienced.

As for the individuals who caused the damage, the above procedure is not always applicable, and not always sufficient. It is not applicable when there is no identifiable victim of a particular deed, for instance in the case of tax evasion or, from a different perspective, drug dealing. It is insufficient where it does not bring about any change in the psychological attitude that led to the offence. In the first case, a possible process could involve the whole community as the victim which could then be represented by someone who was particularly affected by the violation, despite the fact that no clear correlation may exist between the disadvantage or stress situation and the infringement. Adhering to the models mentioned above, reconciliation and mediation could be used for those who were unable to access adequate services for lack of public funds, or for people who are following detox treatment. Or another road could be a confrontation taking place between the offender and professionals specialising in reconciliation.

In the latter case that is, when the psychological attitude of the offender does not change, the process can be very long – even endless. As long as there is a risk that the fundamental rights of other people might be endangered, it is necessary that those who have violated the norm be put in a situation where they cannot cause further harm. This can also entail the limitation of their personal freedom of movement, and their physical separation from the rest of society.

18.   Limits to Personal Liberty

We can now return to the objection raised in previous pages, namely that life together could not be organised without admitting that, at least occasionally, the fundamental rights of individual members of the community must be compromised, including the basic right to personal liberty.

Now, within the perspective and context of a society which is organised according to different tenets and with different points of reference, this issue is drastically reduced.

The question is, in principle, to check whether a detention facility can be utilised not to inflict a punishment, nor for retributive purposes, or general prevention, but only to neutralise those individuals who, if they were to be reintegrated into society, would continue to attack the rights of other people. These are isolated cases, in which separation is qualitatively different from imprisonment: it only entails the physical hindrance from doing further harm and is instrumental to the rehabilitation of the person, which remains the primary objective of any intervention.

Respect for the dignity of a human being requires that such a restrictive measure as the deprivation of personal liberty be allowed only when fundamental rights of equal or higher importance are threatened. Following this approach, the respect for dignity does not tolerate suffering as an end in itself, nor as a consequence of retributive demands. The duration of limits on freedom should be proportional to the requirements of rehabilitation, rather than to the seriousness of the offence, and neutralisation cannot limit personal rights that do not clash with community protection.

It is no use hiding the fact that moving from a sanction system to a rehabilitation system requires time and modulation. The process, however, must follow a set of tenets.

Neutralisation must be carried out using measures different from detention whenever they suffice. Even when there is no alternative, a limitation on personal liberty must respect the dignity of the individual.

As a consequence, the conditions of imprisonment cannot entail the degradation, either physical or psychological, of those incarcerated.

Therefore detention in overcrowded facilities is not allowed. Emotional relationships cannot be severed or limited except for organisational reasons, or in order to protect the community effectively. Education and work must be the norm. The health of the convict has to be guaranteed just like that of people at liberty. Discipline inside the facility must conform to the principles that govern society in general. The legal capacity of the convict cannot be restricted, except when necessary to prevent the convict from committing further offences, or achieving the same ends pursued with previous violations.

At the same time, not only is the use of reconciliation and reparation measures typical of the horizontal society to be progressively increased, but reliance on criminal trials has to be gradually reduced, because in many respects they seem hardly compatible with the horizontal model of social organisation.

19. Vertical Society, Horizontal Society, Ideology and Religion

People often think of right-wing ideologies as promoting a vertical social structure, whereas left-wing movements tend to pursue a horizontal organisation – a paradigm that is also suggested by Christianity, which is the most widespread religion in the civilisation we belong to.

It is indeed characteristic of the right that they organise society into a pyramid, on the basis that it is natural to use human beings as instruments. There is no need to enter into any detail to show this; it is enough to go through the history of the last two centuries to realise that the rise of personal rights in several parts of the world coincided with the overcoming of radical right-wing regimes. Yet it must be noted that, in various instances, the vertical paradigm is strongly mitigated by aspects of solidarity which bring some societies governed by the right close to situations that are typical of the horizontal organisation.

It is also true that right-wing ideology envisages a hierarchically modelled society, characterised by unequally distributed rights and duties, and a lack of guarantees for people living in the lower segments of society. But it does sometimes happen that outspokenly right-wing governments abolish the death penalty, protect some basic rights, take special care of health and education, and address labour issues in terms of worker guarantees and not just productivity demands. In short, the right-wing organisation of society culturally tends towards verticality, while yet in practice, it can detach itself considerably from its original paradigm, sometimes achieving an organisation that does not differ significantly from that of societies which do not identify with a right-wing ideology.

On the other side, there is a somewhat widespread belief that left-wing ideology is based on the recognition of individuals and the protection of their fundamental rights. Whether this belief is true or false, the application of the left-wing organisational model has in general led to diametrically opposed results, in particular in 'Real Socialism' regimes: deportations, massacres, significant restrictions to personal liberty and freedom of thought, intolerance of other people's views, and the creation of hierarchies that were essentially identical to those existing in countries ruled by the most radical right. In short, very often the basis of a social organisation, even in a left-wing context, has been the idea of the individual as instrument – which generates a vertical organisation of society.

So called 'centre positions' are by definition a blend of both ideas. This is why they show traits of both models, and in some cases turn out to be schizophrenic, ambiguous, inconsistent, and contradictory. This is, however, not infrequently also true of radical right- and left-wing positions.

Governments of opposite political orientations have practiced colonialism, albeit under different names, mass extermination, exploitation of labour, restriction or suppression of freedom of thought and religion, and imperialism. A note to younger readers: colonialism consists in permanently occupying foreign nations, claiming that the invasion is legitimate because it aims at educating, 'redeeming', or even 'freeing' the inhabitants of the country invaded, when the actual intention carried out is the exploitation of its resources and subjugation of its citizens.

As for the religion that is closest to us, Christianity, we can find in it different aspects of both conceptions.

As was mentioned above, Scripture contains references to diametrically opposed models of justice, typical of both the vertical and horizontal society. In practical fact we have the Crusades proclaimed and fought, expeditions which were justified by the claim that Christians wanted to free the Holy Land from the 'infidels' (the very term suggesting that they were denied the dignity Christians were entitled to), but were in fact dictated (according to many) by commercial, economic, and hegemonic plans. The Inquisition was devised and put into practice, with thousands of people tortured and immolated for connection with the devil and for heresy. The Church blessed totalitarian regimes that annihilated all freedoms – for instance, the Church's position on Spanish dictator Franco and on the Chilean leader, Pinochet, was well-known – thereby indicating that it shared that cultural model according to which the person was a mere instrument.

The fact that, at the same time, Christianity has given us Francis of Assisi, Lorenzo Milani, Theresa of Calcutta, and many others, whose work shows that we can attach value to individuals regardless of the nature of their relationship with God, does not diminish the opposite position.

This is also due to the fact that for centuries the Church itself, as a secular institution with a rigidly hierarchical structure, has modelled itself on the paradigm of the vertical society. Just think of the obligation of obedience (which means giving up, or controlling, one's ideas in function of the supremacy of thought granted to the senior in the hierarchy), and the continuing tendency of the Church to impose its own truths on others.

The impossibility of establishing a clear link between the two ideologies, between religious belief and this or that way of considering the individual (and, as a consequence, the impossibility of legitimising one or the other model of social organisation) is a source of confusion and uncertainty. This in turn, albeit under various guises and mystifications, ultimately encourages adherence to a simpler, more instinctive model – that of the vertical society.

All this happens despite the knowledge that it is precisely the radicalisation of this model, which the world largely experienced in the first half of the past century, which led the community of citizens one step away from repudiating it.

The view of the individual as a mere instrument actually constituted the cultural background, the way of understanding relationships, the criterion to identify points of reference, that paved the way for the World Wars, the Shoah, the use of the atomic bomb, and the tragedies and dramas that accompanied these events.

Part III
Towards a Horizontal Society

20. An Attempt to Justify Law at the End of the Second Millennium

Coming out of the disaster of World War II, the international community tried to create, when it was able to behold the tragedy that had occurred, the basic conditions to prevent a recurrence of the dramatic events that had unfolded up to then.

At the end of 1948, the General Assembly of the United Nations proclaimed the Universal Declaration of Human Rights. The Preamble emphasises the connection with a very recent past:

> ... recognition of the inherent dignity and of the equal and inalienable rights of all members of the human family is the foundation of freedom, justice and peace in the world. ... Disregard and contempt for human rights have resulted in barbarous acts which have outraged the conscience of mankind.

The Preamble also stresses the need to transpose a series of general principles into the content of laws:

> It is essential, if man is not to be compelled to have recourse, as a last resort, to rebellion against tyranny and oppression, that human rights should be protected by the rule of law. ... The peoples of the United Nations have in the Charter reaffirmed their faith in fundamental human rights, in the dignity and worth of the human person and in the equal rights of men and women and have determined to promote social progress and better standards of life in larger freedom. ... Member States have pledged themselves to achieve, in co-operation with the United Nations, the promotion of

universal respect for and observance of human rights and fundamental freedoms. ... A common understanding of these rights and freedoms is of the greatest importance for the full realisation of this pledge.

The articles that make up the Declaration identify the fundamental rights of the individual. Given that "all human beings are born free and equal in dignity and rights ... without distinction of any kind, such as race, colour, sex, language, religion, political or other opinion, national or social origin, property, birth, or other status", the Declaration recognises that everyone "has the right to life, liberty and security of person." It states that no one can be reduced to, or held in, slavery; that all are equal before the law, and it asserts that everyone has the right to freedom of thought, conscience and religion, and to peaceful association. It claims that everyone has the right to own property, to work, to a family, to rest, medical care, and education.

Unfortunately these are merely suggestions. The UN General Assembly proclaimed the Declaration "as a common standard of achievement for all peoples and all nations, to the end that every individual and every organ of society, keeping this Declaration constantly in mind, shall strive by teaching and education to promote respect for these rights and freedoms and by progressive measures, national and international, to secure their universal and effective recognition and observance, both among the peoples of Member States themselves and among the peoples of territories under their jurisdiction." They are therefore recommendations. They do not have the force to compel individual member states of the United Nations to apply them: that their laws do not run counter to the Declaration remains a desideratum.

There was no way (or no will) to go further, but nevertheless a principle was introduced. The disasters and evils committed by the human race in the first half of the century persuaded the international community that it was necessary to anchor laws to a set of higher-level tenets.

Albeit only in principle, it was stated that only what is in keeping with the Universal Declaration of Human Rights – and never something that contradicts it – can become the content of a right which can be converted into law.

21. The Limits of International Rules

The principles stated in the Universal Declaration of Human Rights lay the foundation for a horizontal type of society: the person cannot be regarded as a means to an end. On the contrary, individuals are the end, and must be guaranteed the right to life and liberty, that is, to lead a decent life and foster their freedom.

The Declaration stemmed from the strong beliefs of the people who adopted it – of the whole world in some respects – and who had learned from the experiences of those immediately preceding years.

It was, however, a very novel way of thinking, for until then in history, trampling on the individual had been the rule. In order for this way of thinking to take root, it was necessary to act, to change things, to make an effort to give up so many privileges and positions of supremacy that were still in place.

In the United States slavery had been abolished some 80 years before, but black people were still strongly discriminated against and treated as if they were a lesser species. Schools for white children were segregated from those for children of colour. Blacks were not allowed to take seats reserved for white people on public transport, and those who refused to comply could be arrested. The differences between the public lavatories for blacks and those for whites were humiliating. In South Africa there was apartheid: blacks and, from a certain point on, Asians too, were segregated in special areas, such as townships, cities – or better, ghettos – which lacked even the most basic of services. They were subject to restrictions on education, on the use of public services, and so on. Almost all African states were still European colonies. Conservative tendencies from the past and attempts at changing things with violence made it extremely difficult really to put the Universal Declaration of Human Rights into practice by moving resolutely from a vertical towards a horizontal society. And the fact that, as we have seen, the Universal Declaration of Human Rights is not a 'law', and hence does not compel states to adhere faithfully to it when managing their own internal norms and conduct, has been clearly of no help in overcoming difficulties.

However, even if the Declaration had been a 'law', it would have been very hard to apply it without the spontaneous, voluntary adherence of each of the states to which it was addressed. International law often succumbs to the power of individual governments, and cannot compel everyone to comply, especially states which are economically or militarily more powerful.

The reasons which had led to that affirmation, in such a conspicuous way, of the existence of inalienable rights were soon forgotten. Apparently, humankind cannot keep alive the memory of its history, of the things it did, inflicted, or suffered, except for a very short period of time.

Despite the reflections that led to the drafting of the Universal Declaration of Human Rights, despite its adoption and the solemn pledge of so many nations to avoid the reinstitution – or the persistence – of social models that could again endanger the life and freedom of people, very soon that sparkle of an equal distribution of benefits and burdens, which seemed to be everybody's wish, once again turned into an almost forced march towards an unequal, discriminating society (especially in regard to the interaction between states and their citizens), in which international and personal relationships are modelled on the structure of a vertical society.

It is worth asking once again why, after the end of the World Wars, after the Shoah and the atomic bombs, the international community (manifesting for the first time its will to break loose from the past) decided to identify a set of founding rules which could form the basis for our living together. It is worth asking why it happened at that particular point in history.

I believe the answer lies in the fact that the tragedy had just ended. People, individuals, had suffered personally those atrocities, tragedies, losses, discriminations, and abuses. Many of them still bore the marks of them on their skin, many more in their hearts: parents who had lost their children, sisters who had lost their brothers, children who had lost their parents. And then there was the feeling of repulsion, sometimes of guilt, for what had happened to a friend or a neighbour. And the vision of entire cities razed to the ground, the memory of life as evacuees or refugees, of living far away from the reference points and connections to your identity.

The memory was alive, so alive that the spirit rebelled against such wreckage, against the feelings of uncertainty and uneasiness felt by each and every human being. At the time, a sense prevailed that each individual would only be protected if the others, all the others, had been protected. People still had in their eyes the vision of apocalypse, and upon the ashes of a world based on inequality and disproportion they tried to erect a new project. And because of the very experiences they had just gone through, such a project could only start from a recognition of the fundamental rights of everyone.

The passing of time, however, clouds memory to the point of erasing it.

22. An Attempt at Creating a Horizontal Society: the Italian Constitution

Even before the Universal Declaration of Human Rights was proclaimed worldwide, in Italy the Constitution – inspired by the same beliefs – came into force.

A constitution is that set of regulations which establishes the principles governing relationships between people, determining the model for the organisation of society, and identifying mandatory, inviolable, inalienable rights and inescapable duties. It is a fundamental law that shapes all the other norms issuing in a state. It performs more or less the same function as natural right did in the past, when laws were regarded as just (or unjust) insofar as they were in keeping with (or in opposition to) natural right. Similarly, laws today are legitimised by their conformity to the Constitution.

Thus we have come back to evaluating law, not on the basis of its source (which, however, remains a precondition since law can only be enacted by the institutions authorised to do so), but on the basis of its content.

The difference is that, today, content is determined by an agreement among all citizens.

The assembly appointed to draft the Constitution was elected by universal suffrage, that is with the votes of both men and women (who until then had been excluded from elections) on 2 June 1946, the same day that Italian citizens, in a referendum, chose the republic as the form of government for their state, thus abolishing the previous monarchical structure. On 27 December 1947 the Constitution was enacted, and on 1 January 1948 it came into force.

Italy had recently emerged from Fascism, which was modelled on the principles of vertical societies where a few individuals had the power to influence the lives of many. In the Fascist era there were plenty of instances of vertical organisation. They included the abolition of all political parties and labour unions other than the Fascist party and union (which Italian citizens were virtually forced to join; the very few who refused were isolated from society), and consequently the abolition of the freedom of expression, of association, of assembly, of expressing political ideas other than those of the regime. 'Confinement', a police measure introduced in 1926, forced people who were regarded as 'dangerous for the national order of the state' (namely political opponents) to live in isolation, in a *'comune'*, mostly on a small island from which they were unable to leave. The racial laws of 1938 introduced discrimination against 'individuals of Jewish race', imposing a series of prohibitions that degraded them to a very low level in the social hierarchy, until ultimately they were expelled from the community of citizens.

Having just emerged from Fascism and the war, the Constituent Assembly was faced with a situation worse than the one the United Nations would later articulate. Italy had effectively contributed to the disasters inflicted on the whole world. It was also a question of accepting responsibility for the crimes against humanity committed under the Fascist regime. This also explains why the stance taken by the Italian Constitution was far more determined and uncompromising than that in the Universal Declaration.

23.   The Person Comes First

That the choice of the Constituent Assembly tended towards the horizontal model of society is evident. The overall structure of the Constitution was built around the recognition of the value and dignity of the person.

Since *each and every* person embodies value, "the Republic recognises and guarantees the inviolable rights of the person, both as an individual and in the social groups where human personality is expressed. The Republic expects that the fundamental duties of political, economic and social solidarity be fulfilled." And in order to be equally protected, "all citizens have equal social dignity and are equal before the law, without distinction of sex, race, language, religion, political opinion, personal and social conditions." This is not a statement of principle, but a justiciable law, a pledge that binds institutions. Indeed, "it is the duty of the Republic to remove those obstacles of an economic or social nature which constrain the freedom and equality of citizens, thereby impeding the full development of the human person and the effective participation of all workers in the political, economic and social organisation of the country." This is exactly the opposite of a vertical society, based on an unequal distribution and the reduction of the individual to an instrument.

The principles contained in these regulations (articles 2 and 3) are the cornerstone of the Constitution. All the rest (originally 139 articles, five being repealed in 2001 by a constitutional revision concerning federalism) represent a definition, in terms of content or form, and an explanation of those founding principles.

After recognising the existence of indefeasible, inalienable, inviolable rights, the Constitution subsequently addresses their definition. This is a crucial step because their number and quality determine to what extent the organisation of life in common is oriented towards the horizontal model of society.

If fundamental rights are weak, if they are badly defined, then a Parliament having a plan to enact laws which restrict the freedoms and the prerogatives of certain sectors of the population will not encounter major obstacles. This is why a defining part of the fundamental bill of rights addresses the definition and description of the indefeasible rights of everyone, among them, the right to personal liberty, freedom of thought, freedom of movement, freedom of religion, work, medical care, and education.

From the perspective adopted by the Assembly, war is not allowed as a means to attack someone else's liberties or to solve international controversies. The word used by the Constituent Assembly is 'to repudiate', a term that is inordinately more radical than all its synonyms, and leaves no room for loose or lenient interpretations.

The Constitution also establishes the limits to fundamental rights. For example, after having recognised the right of association, it forbids secret associations and those which pursue political ends through military-like organisations.

Fundamental rights are substantive, but that substantiveness can be marred, or even annihilated, by form. Therefore, in order to avoid this, the Constitution specifies the forms – the procedures, methods, systems – through which the institutions (or 'power') manage themselves and relate to citizens, and they in turn relate to each other.

For fundamental rights to be guaranteed, for everybody to be equal before the law, and avoiding that certain categories, groups, or subjects are given special treatment, whether privileged or punitive, it is necessary to define the organs of state and the limits to what they do and how they do it.

Consequently, the Constitution establishes how the Parliament is composed, how long its members remain in office, its functions, and the procedures to issue new laws. The same is specified for the government, the judiciary, the constitutional court, and the other constitutionally relevant institutions.

Regarding the judiciary, its independence is especially protected, given its pivotal role in the practical application of the principle of the separation of powers.

An example can help us understand the importance of procedures. If it were established that all are equal before the law, but a further regulation provided that the public prosecutor is free to investigate (to his liking or following orders from the parliament or government) only certain individuals, not all, who are accused of having committed a crime, the essential principle of equality would be grossly distorted by a procedural rule. Apparently all would be equal, all equally liable to stand trial and, if found guilty, be sentenced. In actuality, only the people whom the judicial authority (be it for political reasons, sex, or social position) chose to investigate would face all of this.

The Constitution is strongly inspired by the horizontal model of society, but it has never entirely coincided with it. For example, until recently, the death penalty was permitted – although only in exceptional situations, that is, in the cases provided for by wartime military laws.

The Catholic Church is given privileged treatment in comparison to all other religious institutions. This clearly contradicts the fundamental rule of the Constitution itself, which states that all are equal before the law, without distinction of, among other things, religion.

24.   What is Missing?

If we wanted fundamental law to be fully consistent with the horizontal society, then other points would need to be modified. More than in their substance (which, anyway, reveals some inconsistencies as we have seen with the treatment of churches), they seem to need updating in some formal aspects, namely the procedures which pertain to the functioning of the institutional organisation.

We have already mentioned that the horizontal way of organising society is particularly complex. A careful balancing of all the different circumstances of people is needed, if the rights of everyone and the equality of each individual before the law are to be guaranteed. The complexity of the system, however, does not mean that the administrative apparatus has to be massively complex. Moreover, institutions have to be as transparent as possible if the choices of citizens and control of those are to be effective.

In view of full achievement of the horizontal society, a constitutional law which immediately granted citizenship to all people born in Italy, and the right to vote to foreigners who have fixed their residence in Italy, would lead to a more extensive recognition of the fundamental rights of everybody. Measures such as the reduction in the number of members of Parliament (now 630 in the lower house and 315, plus some lifelong members, in the Senate) and the abolition of provinces (which, with the Regions functioning properly, would hardly find any specific sphere of competence) would streamline the institutional apparatus, thus reducing the burden citizens have to bear to support it.

Abandoning the principle of a symmetrical bicameral mechanism – whereby the same bill has to be passed by both chambers in order to become a law – could result in greater efficiency. Assigning more responsibility to political parties in terms of financing and transparency would make it easier for citizens to obtain important information for exercising their voting rights more consciously.

A reflection on the changing times is also essential. Did the 60 years which have elapsed since the Constitution entered into force influence its efficacy in regard to the actual protection of the personal rights of all, considering the new organisations, visions, and subjects that have emerged on the social scene?

Are the traditional tripartite system and the separation of powers, proposed by Montesquieu, still enough to guarantee the exercise of the fundamental rights of the person, given the growing importance of information on the one hand, and of economy and finance on the other?

If citizens cannot adequately inform themselves, their choices will only be apparent, not effective, since they would be misled by the incomplete, inaccurate, or biased accounts of facts they are given. Economy and finance can alter the balance of the social model in many ways. They can interact with information by conditioning it; they can interfere with the proper functioning of institutions through corruption, or they can provide a link with pervasive criminal organisations such as the mafia.

Information as we know it was very different only two centuries ago when the separation of powers was proposed – or even 60 years ago when the Constitution came into force. In the 18th century the division of powers itself was but a hypothesis about the future, and in an even more distant future one could hypothesise the foundation of a legislative body elected directly by the vote of all citizens without distinction in sex.

The hypothesis that correct information about facts, responsibilities, entanglements, hidden agendas, might be an essential premise for attentive voting could have been made, but it certainly had no particular influence on the reality of that time.

The situation was certainly different some 60 years ago, but not so different as to change substantially the importance of information. The circulation of news had improved thanks to newspapers; the radio had been invented, and its voice entered directly into the homes of citizens, delivering information, sometimes in real time, even to those who could not read. Nevertheless the literacy percentage was still low, and the radio was not very widespread, especially among poorer people. Television had not yet been introduced into Italy, although it would later become the most powerful, and by far most persuasive, medium for spreading information.

Back then, people did not fully realise yet to what extent the power of the media could affect the choices of citizens. Neither did they fully grasp how much money could affect the correct functioning of society, even as it strived for a 'horizontal' model in terms of organisation and of the distribution of rights and opportunities.

Given this change of picture, it would be appropriate to modify the Constitution, introducing regulations to guarantee an effective plurality of information for citizens. It would become mandatory to guarantee its neutrality with respect to the other powers of the state, and to economy and finance, ensuring that they do not exert undue pressure on the administration of society.

To sum up, for the organisation system of Italian society to coincide with the horizontal model, a few adjustments to the Constitution would be necessary, as well as a thorough adaptation of ordinary legislation to those constitutional principles, and the introduction of measures to prevent newer powers from causing dangerous interferences with traditional powers or unduly influencing them.

All this would still not be enough to implement the model of horizontal society, because laws in themselves are not enough to achieve civilised life in common. In fact, as will be explained in the following pages, a significant role is also played by personal beliefs and conduct.

25. Uncertainties in the Constitutional Process

Enforcing the Constitution was not an easy task. The Constitutional Court, which since the beginning should have had the basic task of reviewing laws for legitimacy, was only established in 1953. The *Consiglio Superiore della Magistratura* (or CSM, the magistrates' governing council), whose task is to guarantee the independence of judges and public prosecutors from the other powers of the state, was created in 1958. The regions (a form of devolution and more direct democracy) have only existed since 1970; the same year saw the enactment of the Statute of Labourers, the law that adapts labour legislation to constitutional principles. And in order to harmonise marriage legislation with the equality principle we had to wait until 1975.

It was not easy, because resistance to adjust laws – and behaviour all the more so – to the Constitution was strong, widespread on all levels, and unrelenting.

The typical culture of the vertical society, already deeply rooted before the Fascist era, and animated by that regime, could not be erased overnight by simply issuing a new constitution. The oligarchic, hierarchic, pyramid-like structure involved a distribution of rights and duties that was grossly unequal in every sector of society.

Think of the relationship between the sexes: in a family, the man was explicitly attributed the role of leader, and the woman had to submit to him. As for politics, women were not allowed to vote, and could not be employed in certain parts of the public administration. The culture and mindset of a substantial part of the citizenry, including sometimes people who were oppressed and penalised, regarded discrimination as 'natural', in keeping with laws and regulations. In such a situation, it is not hard to imagine how strongly the privileged fought against the enforcement of a law that ran contrary to their daily habits.

Despite the passing of time, despite legislative action, which, albeit slowly, successfully adapted the body of laws inherited from Fascism to the new structure; despite the frequent rulings of the Constitutional Court which progressively expelled from the legal system so many laws that clashed with the horizontal model, the new structure never managed to fully establish itself.

Even today, the recognition of fundamental rights for some categories of foreigners is often limited to statements that have no bearing on reality. The sanction system is still tied to the retributive idea of penalty. Criminal law, in its general structure, still dates back to the early 1930s, and it is obviously imbued with the authoritarian culture of Fascism. Housing is not a general right, and the repudiation of war has faltered on many occasions.

Apparently, we are returning to a vertical conception of society, sometimes hastily, and in sectors from which it seemed to have been banned once and for all. Labour is becoming increasingly uncertain, and is losing its character of a right, turning instead into a sort of benign concession. The living conditions of irregular foreigners are getting worse. A repressive system disproportionately penalises repeat offenders and mitigates the consequences of crimes typically associated with powerful people.

The horizontal model, the one that guarantees the universality of fundamental rights and the equality of people, is apparently losing ground as the vertical model, based on social hierarchy, privilege, and discrimination, seems again to prevail more and more frequently.

26. Culture

For many, abandoning the vertical model is not compatible with human nature, and is, at best, utopian. For the reasons explained in the previous pages, reasons which have to do with history, religion, and the instincts of individuals, the vertical model is so deeply ingrained that it appears 'natural', and hence 'just'.

This is a cultural attitude, the same as that which caused torture to appear 'just' some decades before Cesare Beccaria's writings were published.

Because this attitude is widespread, it is also shared by many who do not occupy high places in the social hierarchy, especially when they exercise some sort of power, even a modicum of it, on those yet below them (for instance, on irregular foreigners, but also by husbands on wives who have no income of their own). Sometimes this attitude may even be shared by the 'victims' themselves.

The order of things that everyone already finds pre-established, coupled with the need for security, the glorification of sacrifice for the common good, a spontaneous tendency towards submission, and several other factors, leads many to perceive as 'just' the existence of a hierarchy of rights and duties – the fact that someone is in command and others have to obey.

Thus it sometimes happens that the formal system is organised horizontally, that written laws recognise fundamental rights and equality, but at the same time there exists a submerged order, with rules which contradict the 'official' ones, and whose repercussions affect all citizens, ultimately turning the horizontal organisation into a vertical one.

The existence of this phenomenon can sometimes be deduced from a few 'circumstantial' elements. Negligence in the prevention of industrial accidents (which in Italy account for over 1000 'white deaths' per year) is an indicator of the faltering recognition and protection of the right to life and physical integrity for workers, and of the predominance of a submerged rule that gives priority to entrepreneur profit.

Sometimes the visible signs of this double standard, and of the predominance of the submerged one, are blatant. In the early 1990s in Italy, a veritable, pervasive system of corruption was unearthed connecting business and political parties.

The basic rule that (very briefly) contracts for public works are to be awarded to the company that offers the best service at the lowest price, had secretly been replaced in actual practice, and with no apparent change, by a submerged rule whereby the contract was to be awarded to companies which had corrupted public officials and political representatives by paying them bribes for the purpose of winning the contract. This submerged rule was so widespread that over 4000 people – only in the Milan judicial district (among them party leaders, a considerable number of Members of Parliament, a few ministers, former prime ministers, and mayors of big cities) – became involved in investigations.

That this secret anti-established law rule was the actual rule in force can be deduced not only by how frequently it was applied – public contracts were largely accompanied by illegal money movements – but also by the reaction of the political world and of a large number of citizens after the early stages of the investigation.

Within a little more than two years, a series of new laws were enacted which recharacterised some offences, reduced penalties for others, modified several procedural rules making it more difficult to acquire evidence, and introduced new types of trial immunity. In the meantime, nothing was changed in order to make it harder to commit corruption, despite the fact that it was found to be extremely widespread.

Over time the system, which was based on the buying and selling of public offices, was gradually covered by the dust of oblivion until it became almost normal to question its very existence in history. The growth of illegality in the relationships among politics, business, and the economy (a problem having to do with the failure to observe criminal laws, usually described by the euphemism a 'moral question') was removed from collective memory – which shows that the system of rules applied by the institutions in general was the submerged one, and not the official one (even though there were some members of those institutions who held opposing views and behaved appropriately).

A large number of citizens accepted the fading away of this memory, and even actively contributed to it. In the early stages of the investigation, until the circumstances and the evidence gathered led to the involvement of people so powerful that no ordinary citizen could identify with them, the disgust for the illicit behaviour which had just been uncovered was general, and the call for a return to legal conduct was unanimous. Execration of these deeds was repeated daily, and sometimes even led to lack of due respect for some involved in criminal trials.

When trial evidence began to involve ordinary people (tax officers who failed to report tax irregularities in exchange for bribes; officers who neglected to control hygiene in food stores in exchange for free shopping, and such like) the attitude of many changed radically. As people gradually came to realise that anyone could become the object of the public prosecutors' attention in the future, calls for lawful behaviour fell silent.

Another indicator of the predominance of a vertical model underlying the purported horizontal model is also Parliament's habit of passing acts of pardon. The history of the Italian republic is filled with building and tax amnesties, pardons, and general amnesties. These measures allow citizens to amend irregular situations through the payment of money, or even to avoid a penalty altogether.

The precondition for these measures is mass transgression. If only a few citizens failed to pay taxes, built in forbidden areas, or committed crimes, these pardons would have no reason to exist. There would be a lack of raw material. Frequent amnesties and pardons are the proof that the rules of privilege and abuse are applied despite the equality laws formally in force.

Another symptom of the general consensus on vertical culture is the relationship citizens have with their institutions, one often characterised by the belief that they are still subjects.

When a culture is imbued by verticality and hierarchy, citizens see institutions as the expression of an arbitrary power, rather than the fulfilment of a service function. Arbitrary power can do whatever it wants, and citizens must submit to it. Malfunction, but also abuse, are accepted with resignation and fatalism, as if they were an inevitable implication of dealing with institutions. Of course everybody remains entitled to their 'right to grumble', to whine in order to express discontent – sometimes the whining turns into a clearly perceptible complaint that fills the air. However, this grumbling is unlikely to make a qualitative leap, to go from the defeatist complaint of a subject to the proactive request for an assumption of specific responsibilities that is the prerogative of a citizen.

Those who, on the other hand, believe they occupy higher levels of the social ladder by reference to a social hierarchy that exists apart from public institutions, tend to snub those who on the lower levels represent these institutions. "Don't you know who I am?" is an expression that best describes this mentality. Those who apply it hearken back to a model of relating to others in which the rules of the horizontal society succumb to the hierarchy of power. Translated into less coarse words, this remonstration "Don't you know who I am?" would sound more or less like, "Maybe you are not well informed: I am someone important, I am close to the top of this society. The rules you are referring to, which you think forbid me from this (for instance using a car in a pedestrian area), or require me to do something different from what I am doing now (for instance, paying taxes), well these rules apply to others, who live on lower levels of society. But they are not valid for me."

Arrogance is a frequent attitude, as is subjection. In general both attitudes are found in the same person, who is arrogant to those below and submissive to those above.

From another viewpoint, this turns out to be the same (typically, but not exclusively, Italian) phenomenon that often leads to debates on lawful behaviour and complaints that rules are not respected.

Most of the time we blame others for their behaviour, but when it comes to judge ourselves in relation to our ability to observe rules, this attitude is reversed. Everyone claims the right to check whether the rule applies to him or her in that specific case or if an exception can be made. To have a small but significant affirmation of this, just look at the reaction of people who find a car parked in front of their driveway, and then compare that to the justifications they give when they leave their own car parked in front of the main door of someone else's house.

27. The Interests of Those Who Oppose the Horizontal Society

One way in which history develops is through painful, not always consistent, progress towards the recognition of the other, regardless of contingent events. Of course lapses and regressions have been frequent and significant, but I think it is undeniable that, in general, the ability to see a fellow person in the other has gradually spread. This is the precondition to imagining a truly horizontal organisation.

The horizontal society is opposed by interests of various natures. First and foremost, as we mentioned, resistance comes from people who have access to positions of privilege and wish to preserve them. The drive to do so is strong, even when it threatens their peace of mind and future.

The appeal of privilege, of course, is not exclusively rooted in the personal advantages it brings. Anyone would prefer to live in a comfortable apartment, to use means of transportation that are fast, always available, and can avoid traffic jams; to be treated medically in the shortest possible time by the best doctors, rather than experience the opposite. Everyone cares for their own well-being and, when the latter derives from a situation of privilege, they tend to hold on to such privileges in order not lo lose that level of well-being. Therefore there is a widespread, selfish interest in preserving the vertical society when this is instrumental to maintaining a situation of well-being that results from privilege and unequal distribution.

This interest, however, also involves other factors that have to do with instinct, or the irrational part of the individual. It has to do with the perception of having the power to do what others cannot do, the feeling of being different from all the others, and the satisfaction derived from it. Privilege does not only entail the ability to satisfy better and more easily one's need for well-being. It also delineates clearly recognisable differences between one's own limits and those allotted to others whose standing is clearly lower, subordinate. This need for constant comparison between one's own privileges and the disadvantages of others is due to the fact that people are constantly competing, and take the place they hold in the hierarchical social scale as the sole yardstick of self-evaluation.

Realising that one is privileged is, at the same time, also a powerful way of mystifying reality and pretending that you are really different from other people. The distinction which comes from power, predominance, and arbitrariness can delude people into believing that they are similar to god: all-powerful and eternal.

28. Security

From the same perspective, privilege is fascinating because it gives a feeling of security. So as to avoid fear, human beings would almost be willing to die. They are certainly willing to give up a substantial portion of their freedom.

They accept being monitored by surveillance cameras in each and every public place, and allow their privacy to be restricted by dozens of other intrusions. They install alarm systems, armoured doors, iron bars, turning their houses into what looks like a prison – difficult to enter, but sometimes also difficult to leave.

Increasingly, fear becomes a tool for political use. The promise of freedom from fear attracts votes, because fear rises from the gut, not the brain, and so hardly lends itself to rational discussion.

The perception of insecurity can be enhanced and artfully steered by filtering information, fuelling fear, emphasising the more upsetting aspects, so that the promise to make people secure becomes even more attractive.

The results of statistical surveys are not important. Although it can be demonstrated that we more frequently are the victims of aggression by relatives, friends, or acquaintances, what creates terror are strangers, the different people who come from afar. They are the ones who scare citizens, and it is with reference to them that security is discussed. Fear divides, erecting barriers against foreigners. It hinders recognition, fostering the basic beliefs on which vertical societies rest. What cannot be overlooked on a global view, is the fact that the closer one gets to the top of the pyramid, the more a society tends to protect security. Members of the government are surrounded by people whose only task is to take care of the politicians' security.

If you examine the statistics however, workers in the building sector would be much more in need of an armed escort.

The desire for privilege, difference, and security pushes people to shamelessly engage in unrestrained competition. Thus they enter a vicious circle, an endless race towards asserting their superiority, without accepting limits – not even the need to preserve natural resources, which in the long run jeopardises the survival of humankind itself.

29. Escaping Responsibility

One further factor that contributes to the vertical structuring of society is the tendency blindly to delegate personal involvement and commitment.

In a broad, complex society, the mechanism of delegating to representatives functions that cannot be directly exercised by everybody is inherent in its normal functioning. But this process is only justified if it is strictly limited to the functions whose nature requires representation, and if it includes mechanisms to control how it is actually carried out.

However, it often happens that the responsibility of the individual gets 'shifted' to others, without caring about the use they will make of it.

This mechanism also applies to the exercise of critical thinking, which means checking facts, information, statements, behaviours, and consistency. When people are not completely careless, they might choose a person who is already known for some reason, turn them into a 'myth', and charge them with the task of not only controlling, but also severely criticising power. They have attributed to them the role as collective conscience, and sometimes people gather to listen to them, almost as in a rite. On such occasions, some people temporarily experience strong feelings of resentment and aggressiveness towards the 'evil' people who manage power; others become indignant, or lash out at them. Then, little by little, they return to their private lives, leaving it to the myth, the 'guru' to think and act, even for them.

People tend to take this attitude not just because it is often more comfortable, but also because responsibility has a price. At first it generates uncertainty, second thoughts, doubts, and later regrets, recrimination, and guilt. If decisions are delegated to others, individual responsibility disappears. Despite these apparent advantages, however, the damage is huge. If people put their destiny into the hands of others, their delegates will not shape it according to the goals and interests of the people who chose them, but according to their own interests, or those of their political, ideological, or religious faction. In short, if you let others do the job, they will act according to their own approach, goals, and in their own interest.

Blank delegation of responsibility, disinterest, and the resulting indifference, are in keeping with the vertical model, indeed they often contribute to implement it, for delegation, disinterest, and indifference lead to the establishment of hierarchies, and these in turn involve an unequal distribution of rights and duties.

Another factor that contributes to the vertical organisation of society is the tendency to avoid accountability for one's own actions, when these are carried out upon advice, or order, of a higher authority of whatever kind.

In 1961, at Yale University, Stanley Milgram tested how far individuals would go in inflicting suffering on their fellows when responsibility could be shifted to someone else. His experiment consisted in delivering electric shocks of increasingly high voltage to people who were unable to memorise, and hence repeat, a series of verbal associations. The justification Milgram gave for the inflicted pain was scientific: giving the electric shocks served to check whether the pain inflicted would help memorisation. Any doubts were answered by reassuring participants about the 'authority' of the experiment-leader. A wall between the two people (which allowed them to hear but not see) served to abate the intensity of the relationship between the performer of the experiment and the victim. Two thirds of the participants went as far as delivering shock doses of electricity (450 volts), despite being aware of the 'pain' they were causing. An actor played the victim's part, behaving as if he were really suffering from the shocks, whereas those who were administering the shocks believed everything was real.

Two out of three people, therefore, decided that it was all right to inflict severe, even life-threatening, pain on their fellows. This means they were willing to reduce other people to instruments, only because this 'instrumentalisation' was justified by its alleged scientific utility. We are reminded of the criminal, inhumane experiments performed by Joseph Mengele and his associates on people, including children, who were interned in Nazi concentration camps.

Other similar experiments have confirmed a widespread willingness in people to harm others when they feel psychologically freed from taking responsibility for their behaviour, because responsibility falls on third parties for reasons that have ultimately to do with hierarchy. It is from this perspective that many senior Nazis, figures accused of the most heinous atrocities during the trials brought against them, defended themselves by claiming they were not responsible for the crimes they were charged with, because they had committed them in compliance with higher orders – and hence had carried out a duty.

This tendency to relinquish responsibility, as well as to delegate blindly, raise questions about the relationship between individuals and freedom. Many people are scared by freedom, because it forces them to make choices. Choosing is complex, difficult: it implies judgements about good and evil (which are not always clearly discernible). Judgements force people to evaluate circumstances, meaning that what is positive in one situation can be harmful in another, and they do not allow for reference paradigms that are valid in just any situation. Choosing causes doubts, anxiety, and insecurity – hence the tendency to escape from freedom and take refuge in arbitrariness (which by definition implies no responsibility) or in submission (which means transferring responsibility to others). Paradoxically, one of the strongest reasons why people resist the creation of a horizontal society lies in the fact that such a society would give them that freedom.

Part IV
How Do We Get There?

30. The Time Dynamic

History is a path; there is a before and an after, a yesterday, a today, and a tomorrow. It is a route, formed by a concatenation of steps. It resembles a long, arduous mountain trail on which you cannot see the end. Each step in itself seems to be unimportant – so short it is compared to the whole length of the way – yet you only realise how important it is when you turn back and notice the distance you have covered, or when you look ahead and start to catch a glimpse of the destination. The perception of history, of the progress of humanity along the way, is not always the same: individual moments and steps are experienced as if they did not have a before and an after, as if people did not understand that reaching the end requires a series of steps, and takes time.

The attitude of people towards history is one of impatience: they want an immediate solution, they demand that changes take place overnight. If they cannot perceive them immediately, they tend to rule out that it can happen. They lose heart and get stuck, like whining children who refuse to keep on walking and expect to be picked up into someone's arms. The great effort they have put into taking each step seems to be wasted, since they are unable see the destination or discern the path.

What is missing is the idea of building, of putting one brick on top of another, so that finally the house can be seen.

Sometimes the prospect that, along the way of history, overcoming injustice may take time seems too hard to accept. Some people may shut themselves off, erasing the issue and living as if the problem did not exist. Others may indulge in violent rebellion. The former lapse into indifference; they leave the scene. The latter are caught in a hopeless spiral, becoming themselves the cause of blatant injustice – reckless, overambitious death-mongers. They can be compared to the judges who impose the death penalty (lawlessly, without a trial, without evidence, without the possibility of defence); abusers of other people's dignity, mirrors that reflect the same intolerant, haughty, and boastful otherness they claim (and sometimes even believe) to fight.

The way towards the horizontal society is also marked by the perception of time, of its dynamic – the hitches, falls, breaks, regressions, and recoveries. Just like on a mountain trail.

To place oneself in time means to have an overview of the past and consider the steps which have already been taken, the differences between today and yesterday. What if the path shows us that horizontal societies have never been experimented with, except occasionally and with no lasting effects? Well, the path also shows us that every step was successful when it was taken at the right pace for its time. Was it impossible that slavery could be rejected at the time of Spartacus? Of course, but that is what happened, two thousand years later. Was it impossible that torture could be repudiated in the Middle Ages? Exactly, but that is what happened in the 18th century. Has it been impossible until now to model ourselves on the forms of the horizontal society? No doubt. However, just like other epoch-making upheavals that have become possible – but were unthinkable before – it may well be that the time is finally ripe for recognising and accepting, instead of rejecting, each other.

Some experiences from the recent past (the nonviolent revolution of Mohandas Karamchand Gandhi, the South African reconciliation with Nelson Mandela, the bloodless end of the dictatorships in Greece, Spain, and Portugal, and the disintegration of the Soviet Union) are signals of this change which should not be underrated.

31. Self-Awareness

There are people who claim they share a belief in the organisation system of the horizontal society, but in fact are in no way confident that it can be attained. The result is that they consciously accept some, even major, aspects of the vertical model.

The horizontal society presupposes a recognition of and respect for your own value and dignity, as well as of those of others. This implies the awareness that you can be the author of a new society.

During the public meetings I happen to participate in, I often direct people's attention to the responsibility of individual citizens in the malfunctioning of justice. Often times, people express a lack of confidence in their own potential, and I am asked, as if the implicit answer were 'no', whether individuals can have access to the means of enforcing legality, and what these means are. The feeling of one's own importance is expressed very clearly. 'How can you teach young people to respect rules in a world where mass media, and often the family itself, sometimes colleagues, are spreading a culture of the exact opposite?' teachers ask. 'How can I educate my children to follow rules when, taking a look around themselves, they see that connections in high places and arrogance prevail?' parents ask. 'How can I persuade myself to keep being respectful and uncompromising when I see that this brings me disadvantages, while people who deceive and fail to respect others always win?' ask citizens from all social backgrounds.

Sometimes the question is purely rhetorical: it is simply a way of justifying one's own lack of engagement. 'School, family, television, politics, all the institutions are spreading a way of thinking whereby rules are a surplus that can be disposed of, a burden that only creates obstacles, an unjustified way of restricting freedom. Since all these sources of persuasion are so powerful, widespread, deeply rooted, and convincing, I, as an individual, have no means, cannot do anything: I don't have the power to make a difference. The responsibility is not mine; it belongs to the school, the family, television, politics, and the other institutions. They, not I, should take steps to ensure that rules are respected.'

This attitude of withdrawal, of not taking responsibility as an individual, of delegating others to solve problems – thereby freezing and blocking all activity – can be brought into question by explaining why it is necessary to behave in the opposite way.

The shortest route to get there can be summed up in four words: clarity, consistency, engagement, and participation.

Clarity has to do with deep beliefs. In order not to get disoriented, we need to know what we really want. If your personal point of reference is really the horizontal society, if you are able to recognise the other, if you are willing to put aside your privileges, and make sure they do not jeopardise the fundamental rights of others, then you can contribute to the creation of a horizontal society.

Once you have attained clarity, you need consistency. Consistency has to do with the relationship between what you say and what you do.

Here the focus is legality, the observance of rules. In a country governed by the rules of a vertical society, to act means to work towards changing these rules, modifying, replacing them with others inspired by the dignity of the individual.

In a country that has chosen the horizontal model as its founding principle, to act means to apply the pact upon which society is based. It means infusing rules with your behaviour, your actions, your respect, your everyday gestures, in the awareness that, if the opposite were the case, rules would remain a dead letter. Consistency requires attention and engagement; it requires paying attention to how you behave every day when dealing with family, friends, strangers, institutions, stronger and weaker subjects. It involves doing what you say. It is not always easy to be consistent, and sometimes it can be painful: instincts, feelings, but also a mistaken sense of justice, often clash with common-sense and linear thought patterns. However, the stronger the belief in a common point of departure – the inviolability of the person – the less so will consistency be a burden, and the easier it will be to remedy temporary disruptions.

Respecting others also means respecting yourself, so that every time you degrade a person, or are complicit in their denigration, you yourself are degraded as a result because you are part of the same whole. On the one hand, consistency brings individuals into harmony with their own points of reference, and a practical consequence of this is that they grow accustomed to following rules. On the other hand, consistency is a testimonial: it helps give confidence to the people around us that recognising others and their rights is not a utopian project; it helps those around us believe in the possibility of a different way of living together. And as a corollary of the recognition of the other, consistency involves listening to different opinions, and does not exclude – but actually entails – changing one's points of reference when these turn out to be untenable.

Clarity and consistency are not enough. When we live together it is indispensable to participate in social life. To be willing to take part in it, it is necessary to overcome a lack of confidence in yourself and your actions, and to develop an awareness that the individual matters.

To this end, it is helpful to overcome a fictitious opposition between citizens on the one hand (who cannot do anything) and society on the other, as if the two were separate entities with different natures, as if people and the institutions, people and society did not have anything in common. The opposite is true.

Institutions do not exist without the people who constitute them: the former are made up of people. A school, a hospital, a law court, a city office exist as long as there are individuals who work for them. They exist because there are teachers, doctors, nurses, judges, clerks, attorneys, lawyers, mayors, councillors, advisors, registry officials, technical office employees, local police officers, and so on. They are all citizens; they are all people. And those who interact with the institutions in other ways are people too: students who attend schools, sick people who undergo treatment in hospital, the parties and defendants in court, those who need an official certificate or want to build a home, those who travel by car. The acts performed by the institutions, their quality, their fairness, are the acts, the quality, and the fairness of the citizens who embody those institutions, who act with the authority of those institutions. They reflect their attention and attitude towards others.

How many times do the people who demand the efficiency and good functioning of schools, hospitals, and the justice system, turn out to be teachers, doctors, nurses, magistrates, or clerks? Do they not realise that, although they think they are demanding commitment from an abstract, separate, foreign entity, they are actually – without being aware of it – demanding commitment from themselves?

We are the institutions; so a first answer has to do with the behaviour of individuals, of every single citizen, who gives life to the institutions.

Each citizen can immediately develop the awareness that he or she is contributing to build a horizontal society, as long as each keeps behaving in accordance with the basic principles on which this society rests (and which, as is worth noting, in Italy coincide with the Constitution). Therefore, this means that they should avoid violating or compromising the rights and dignity of others, as well as their equality before the law. The key is to become involved, not to back away; to do and not let be done; to take personal responsibility – which means responding to what you are called upon to do in the social organisation.

Here are some examples. A teacher's responsibility is not limited to communicating information and verifying that these have been learned. First and foremost, a teacher should educate young people to respect others, the other students in particular, and guide them to recognise as their fellows every person with whom they are connected. I do not think it is too far-fetched to wonder whether one of the causes of so-called 'bullying' behaviour has to do with certain (conscious or unconscious) attitudes of teachers, who may pick a scapegoat among the children, on which to vent the negative feelings of the class. Or they may extol the behaviour of famous people whose exploits consist of abusing others. A teacher's responsibility involves their applying the criteria of equality in dealing with all pupils, avoiding all forms of discrimination and partiality (possibly due to the wealth of parents). It involves loyalty to everyone. It involves ensuring relationships with anyone who interacts with young people (colleagues, school principals, janitors, parents) be inspired by the same principles. It involves actions being consistent with words, in the awareness that when the former contradict the latter, these are bound to succumb – with the further consequence of teaching hypocrisy.

Judges and public prosecutors must be very careful to avoid the risk arising from the great powers they have been granted to invade other people's lives. Almost all the actions they perform would amount to a crime if done by an ordinary citizen, or by the same officials while not carrying out their duty. Thus they may feel that they rank higher than other citizens, and could therefore fail to pay enough attention to the fundamental rights, dignity, and equality of anyone involved in a trial.

No stereotypical formulas may be used to justify precautionary measures, whose duration, however, should be kept as short as possible. Hence the need to ensure that everybody's position is quickly clarified in one way (release) or another (conducting the trial), without dead time, except for those prescribed by the criminal law, and to avoid treating those involved in the process like mere office files. This means that the autonomy the Constitution so carefully guarantees must be used in the interest of impartiality, both on the part of the judge and of the public prosecutor. In a horizontal society, public prosecutors, as well as judges, must set themselves the goal of accurately reconstructing the facts and correctly attributing responsibility, which is exactly the contrary of acting for partisan ends. Autonomy must be protected, not only with regard to the other established powers, namely Parliament and the government, but also to the economy, finance, public opinion, and one's own public and private existence – even oneself.

What applies to teachers also applies to judges and public prosecutors. What applies to them also applies to Members of Parliament. What applies to MPs also applies to supermarket salespeople, car-repair mechanics, violin teachers and conductors, journalists and directors of TV channels, entrepreneurs and craftsmen. Minimal differences are the result of slight adjustments to the basic principles which are valid for everybody.

Failing to perceive and appreciate the unity or commonality to the source of these principles does not facilitate the horizontal re-structuring of society. If we construct different ethical codes (namely codes of responsibility) according to different fields of activity (business ethics, the ethics of politics, of justice, school ethics, and so on), we divide society into sectors, hindering mutual recognition and paving the way for the institution of corporations and hierarchies.

On the contrary, the bottom line is that what applies to one applies to everybody – even to bank and insurance clerks, and to whomever operates today in the more or less large private conglomerates that increasingly look like public institutions (with one difference: by nature, corporations are not impartial, since they avowedly pursue the goal of generating profit).

To give a practical example which explains to what extent indifference and conformity (namely a lack of participation and of thoughtful participation respectively) can be an obstacle to the horizontal society, rapidly turning it into something similar to the vertical order, you only need to mention the mafia. The mafia commits crimes of the most different kinds, all aimed, more or less directly, to a disproportionate accumulation of money. In order to come back into legal circulation, this money has to be laundered because its illicit origin obviously cannot be declared. The laundering takes place with the help of different systems, often requiring relationships with lending institutions, finance companies, notaries, real estate owners, firms, and businesses. What of the behaviour of the bank clerk, the finance company employee, and the other actors in this process who adhere to the principles of the horizontal society? How do they behave when they become convinced that the money they are dealing with is the product of mafia crime? So they may lose a client, a job opportunity, see a good deal fall through, but they will not contribute to establishing a criminal society and, at the same time, a vertical social model. But let it suffice for them merely to be indifferent to the source of the money, to think it is none of their business, and the outcome will be exactly the opposite.

Conclusion

Do you remember the imaginary country described in the first pages of this book? The one where subterfuge, cunning, force, dishonesty all triumph behind the appearance of equal laws for everyone and respect for every basic right? The one in which those who adhere to formal laws (they may not necessarily be a small number) are stepped over daily by those who do not respect them?

Can we work out a system to reverse that situation, one which does not involve reversing that culture? And can we imagine that culture can change 'on orders of the authority', which, by the way, is an expression of the same citizenship that promotes itself by breaking the law? Isn't the answer to develop an opposite way in one's private life, and then suggest it to other people, to prove to them that it can be practicable, and at the same time show what are the disadvantages the vertical society brings even to the most cunning, to those who have the most connections, to the strongest and most powerful?

Is it necessary, in order to expose these disadvantages, to recall the need for increasingly ghetto-like ways to defend one's own space and property, for the spread of wars, the progressive destruction of resources, the continuous exclusion of large numbers of people from recognition and harmony, the triumph of division and hatred?

Of course the absolute respect of fair rules will never be universal.

We are, all of us, human beings, carrying with us every day all of our imperfections, and we will never be able to contrive and practice perfect forms of common living.

Of course evil cannot be completely eradicated from history. Human nature itself, in its mortal finitude, is a frequent source of anxiety and suffering. All this cannot be remedied by rules and their observance.

Within these limits, the conscious choice, and its consistent application, to move towards a social model based on the recognition of human beings, determine the direction of our journey and qualify each one of its stations. The more we advance, the more possibilities we get to see ourselves and every other person as subjects, not as objects. To be free and not subdued, citizens and not subjects. It is an endless journey, and one in which being on the road is more important than the destination itself: what counts is how you travel this road, how coherent every single gesture and word is with the final result. It is the journey, not the goal, that fills a person with their own special value and dignity. We are all going down this road, and where it will take us is up to every one of us.

Acknowledgments

For many years an international edition of Gherardo Colombo's book *Sulle regole* has been the earnest wish of Comenius Leergangen. Colombo's inexhaustible plea for the importance of the rule of law for a stable and balanced democratic state, one in which its citizens can learn how to be truly free, and one which can foster once again a real sense of community and ethical self-respect is of the utmost relevance, and worthy to be discussed by as many people worldwide as possible.

Colombo's intention closely tracks the aims and ambitions of the Leadership Courses Comenius organises in Europe, the USA, and China, in which Colombo actively participates. Because of this and out of gratitude for Colombo's influential lectures, Comenius decided to embark on an international edition of *On Rules* in close collaboration with Amsterdam University Press and Feltrinelli Editore, Milan, Italy. From the outset René Foqué and Fred Veerman were strong supporters of this initiative.

This edition of *Sulle regole* would have been inconceivable without the dedicated support of many friends, colleagues, and professionals. At the top of this list is Elisabetta Zoni, who translated Colombo's book with great care and dedication. I would like to thank René Foqué for his eloquent contextualisation of Colombo, his work, and his book *On Rules* in the Introduction, translated by David Haljan. For their indispensable support and advice during the preparation and production of this book I thank Inge van der Bijl and Louise Visser of Amsterdam University Press, as well as Theo Collier and Bianca Dinapoli of Feltrinelli Editore.

By their support for this international edition of *Sulle regole*, the staff, faculty, and alumni of Comenius Leergangen honour

Gherardo Colombo for his critical but constructive engagement in reflecting on fundamental aspects of our democratic society.

October 2015
Pieter-Matthijs Gijsbers
Director Comenius Leergangen